Miracles and Mysteries
in the Bible

Miracles and Mysteries in the Bible

**Bruce Kaye
and John Rogerson**

The Westminster Press
Philadelphia

First edition

Published by The Westminster Press ®
Philadelphia, Pennsylvania

PRINTED IN THE UNITED STATES OF AMERICA

9 8 7 6 5 4 3 2 1

Library of Congress Cataloging in Publication Data

Main entry under title:

Miracles and mysteries in the Bible.
    144p. ; 21cm.
    Includes bibliographical references.
    CONTENTS: Rogerson, J. The supernatural in the Old
Testament.—Kaye, B. The supernatural in the New Testament.
    1. Supernatural in the Bible. I. Rogerson, John
William. The supernatural in the Old Testament. 1978.
II. Kaye, Bruce. The supernatural in the New Testament.
1978.
BS680.S86M57   221.6′8   77-24077
ISBN 0-664-24179-4

CONTENTS

Part Two: NEW TESTAMENT, by Bruce Kaye

PUBLISHER'S PREFACE

Anyone who reads the Bible soon encounters miracle stories and mysteries that are troublesome to the modern reader. Some readers simply accept them because they are in the Bible. Others dismiss them as expressions of a world view that is now passé. Still others find ingenious explanations that rationalize the mystery and explain away the miracle.

The authors of this book take another approach. Rather than ask what happened and how, they ask: What did these stories and events mean to those who told them and preserved them in the Holy Scriptures? What do they tell us about God and his relationship to the world and to people? Is there abiding truth to be found here for us today?

This book combines in a single volume two works that were published separately by the Lutterworth Press, London. John Rogerson's *The Supernatural in the Old Testament* and Bruce Kaye's *The Supernatural in the New Testament* were companion books published in a similar format for the same general readers. Both authors teach at the University of Durham, and both combine a competence in Biblical scholarship with a clear and uncomplicated writing style that makes their work useful to the laity as well as to ministers.

Part One. OLD TESTAMENT
by John Rogerson

I INTRODUCTION

'In the beginning God created the heavens and the earth' (Genesis 1:1). The Old Testament is a book in which we expect to find statements about God. If Genesis 1 worries us at all, it is not because of its claim that the existence of the world is dependent upon God; our worries are much more likely to be concerned with how we reconcile the biblical claims with scientific views about the origin of the universe. But what about the following passages?

> 'But the serpent said to the woman, "You will not die."' (Genesis 3:4)
> 'And he looked, and lo, the bush was burning, yet it was not consumed.' (Exodus 3:2)
> 'And the Lord went before them by day in a pillar of cloud to lead them along the way, and by night in a pillar of fire to give them light.' (Exodus 13:21)
> 'Now the Spirit of the Lord departed from Saul, and an evil spirit from the Lord tormented him.' (I Samuel 16:14)
> 'The jar of meal was not spent, neither did the cruse of oil fail, according to the word of the Lord which he spoke by Elijah.' (I Kings 17:16)

These texts raise a number of different problems for us. Was there a talking serpent in the Garden of Eden, and before it was cursed to go on its belly, did it somehow maintain an upright posture? How could a bush burn without being consumed? Were the Israelites accompanied through the wilderness by a solid, moving pillar of cloud which turned into fire at night? Does God torment people by sending evil spirits into them? How were the cruse of oil and the jar of meal replenished?

We find these passages, and others like them, difficult, not simply *because* they speak of God or the supernatural, but because of the *way* in which they do it. In some cases, the moral implications of texts also raise difficulties for us, as in the passage about the evil spirit from God which tempted Saul.

It would be a mistake to think that it is only recently that religious people have been bothered by such questions. In fact, thoughtful religious people have been bothered by them for probably well over a thousand years! Rabbi Ada ben Minyomi, who probably lived in the 5th century AD, wondered if Elijah was fed not by ravens, as stated in I Kings 17:6, but by two men who were both named 'Raven'.[1] Saadia ben Joseph (882–942) tried to explain the difficulty that appears in Genesis 18, when Abraham addresses one of his visitors as though that visitor were God (verse 3). Saadia argued that the Bible had used a sort of shorthand expression, and that what was meant was that Abraham recognized the visitor to be an angel.[2] Another great Jewish scholar, Maimonides (1138–1204), maintained that Abraham's meeting with the three men (Genesis 18), Jacob's wrestling with the angel (Genesis 32:22–32), Balaam's talking ass (Numbers 22:22–35) and Gideon's fleece (Judges 6:36–40) had all occurred in visions or dreams to the persons involved.[3]

For at least the last two hundred years, many Christian scholars have tried to help readers to understand difficult supernatural passages by giving to the texts a 'natural' and 'reasonable' explanation. The talking serpent has been explained as an ancient Israelite example of the sort of world-wide folk-tale in which animals speak. The burning bush was perhaps a sunset gleaming through a bush. In the case of the pillar of cloud, perhaps an observer saw a whirlwind in the camp and interpreted it as a sign of God's presence, while the origin of the pillar of fire was in the lighted braziers carried at the head of caravans at night. Saul's evil spirit was the ancient Israelite way of describing what we today would call mental illness or depression, and Elijah's miracles are the sort of story about the deeds of holy men that can be found the world over.

In some cases, such explanations have been guesswork, and nothing more. This is the case with the suggestions about the burning bush and the pillar of cloud. The explanations about the talking serpent and Elijah's miracles are not unsupported guesswork but are based on a comparative study of folklore. What is said about Saul's evil spirit *is* unsupported guesswork, though based on the undoubted fact that the ancient Israelites did not have the psychological concepts and vocabulary that we use today.

Some people are undoubtedly deeply offended by attempts to 'explain away' the supernatural elements in the Old Testament. But many other people are grateful for what has been done. The point has at least been acknowledged in such 'explaining away' that belief in God does not in-

[1] Babylonian Talmud, Hullin 5a.
[2] See H. Malter, *Life and Works of Saadia Gaon*, Philadelphia, 1921, pages 107–108.
[3] See *The Guide of the Perplexed*, Part II, Sections 32–48. There are numerous translations of the *Guide*, e.g. by S. Pines, Chicago, 1963.

volve a literalist understanding of the Bible, and that it is permissible to approach the Bible with a questioning, as well as a reverent, attitude of mind.

There is, however, a danger that explanations of the supernatural in 'reasonable' and 'ordinary' terms can go too far. We may throw out the baby with the bath water by making the Old Testament so ordinary and reasonable that we lose sight of all that it says about the mystery and majesty of God. We may come to think of the Old Testament writers not as men of God, with deep spiritual insight, but as naive and prescientific persons who knew no better than to attribute to God what modern science can explain without the need for a God.

It would be foolish for me to claim that I can answer questions and solve problems that have been discussed and written about for a very long time. In the following pages, however, I have tried to give some guidance to teachers, general readers, and perhaps even to clergy, about how we may approach some Old Testament passages which have difficult supernatural elements. The approach is, I hope, both questioning and positive, but aimed at a general readership, and not at my professional Old Testament colleagues. If any of the latter happen to read the book, and find that instead of talking about theophanies and cult traditions I have concentrated on the question 'what really happened?', it is because this last question is the one which usually bothers the general reader most.

The main part of the book is devoted to the exposition of some twenty selected passages from the Old Testament, but it may be helpful if I make clear the principles of my approach.

1. NATURAL AND SUPERNATURAL

Among the definitions of 'supernatural' to be found in the *Oxford English Dictionary* there are the following: 'belonging to a higher realm ... than that of nature' and 'abnormal, extraordinary'. The first definition corresponds roughly to what was written in the first paragraph of the introduction. If we believe in God, we assume that he is not a part of nature, but that he is in some way above it and controlling it; he belongs to a higher realm. Verses such as Genesis 1:1 do not worry us merely because they assert that the world is dependent on a higher 'being', God. We can therefore assume that the general reader is not worried by 'supernatural' in this first sense.

It is with the second sense of 'supernatural' that this book will be largely concerned. We are worried by stories about talking animals, jars

3

of oil that never become empty, and dead persons who are restored to life, because these stories describe what for us is *abnormal* and *extraordinary*. Such stories conflict with our modern belief that the world is essentially orderly, and that this order can be described in terms of 'laws' which abnormal and extraordinary happenings seem to break.

The terms 'natural' and 'supernatural' are not biblical terms, and in their popular use (although not necessarily in their use in traditional theology) they suggest a different understanding of the world from that implied in the Old Testament. Popular use of 'natural' and 'supernatural' implies that nature is a closed system in which God 'intervenes' in events that are abnormal and extraordinary, and it is the extraordinary nature of the events which points to their divine origin. In contrast, passages can be found in the Old Testament which suggest that the Israelites believed that God was responsible for all the *ordinary* processes of nature (see Psalm 104:10–24) and it has been asserted that the Israelites had no concept of miracle in the sense of an abnormal or extraordinary event initiated by God.

However, it may be possible to over-estimate the differences between modern popular thought and Old Testament belief about the world; at all events, the differences must be carefully discussed.

Even if parts of the Old Testament describe God as ordering all the processes of nature, it is still probable that the Israelites recognized order and regularity in nature, and that they carried on their technology on the basis of well-tried rules. Genesis 1:1 ff. implies that at creation, unordered matter was organized into an ordered world, and Genesis 8:22, which promises after the flood that 'while the earth remains, seed time and harvest, cold and heat, summer and winter, day and night, shall not cease' describes observable regularity in nature. The same is true of Psalm 19:1–6, and in Jeremiah 8:7, the prophet contrasts the inconstancy of God's people with the unfailing regularity with which migratory birds journey to and from Judah in due season. In the book of Ecclesiastes, the writer bases some of his apparent scepticism on the regular recurring pattern of events, including events in nature (1:5–7), which he sums up in the observation that there is nothing new under the sun.[4]

Not only can we say that the Israelites recognized order and regularity in nature, but it is clear that they also recognized events that were inconsistent with this regularity and order. They did not expect animals

---

[4] See further the section entitled 'law in the natural process' in W. Eichrodt, *Theology of the Old Testament*, Vol 2, London, 1967, pages 152 ff.

to talk, jars never to be empty, shadows of sundials to go backwards, and dead persons to be restored to life; the whole point about recording the extraordinary achievements of, say, Elijah or Elisha was precisely to emphasize that these men did things that did not happen in the ordinary run of events, and that, therefore, they were special servants of God. In this sense, we could justifiably say that the Israelites did recognize what we would call a miracle (in the sense of something extraordinary or abnormal) even if they had no special word for it.

What we do not know is whether the Israelites had built up a body of abstract theoretical speculation about the order and regularity of the world of nature. Even if they had done so, it is certain that it would have differed from modern theoretical speculation, at least in scope if not more fundamentally. For us today, an eclipse is not an abnormal or extraordinary event; but it was probably just that for ancient Israelites, and if so, to be put in the same category as extraordinary jars of oil and resuscitated corpses. We can conclude that although Israelites, like ourselves, recognized that certain happenings were inconsistent with order and regularity in nature, the Israelite would have included more events in this category than we do. Also, he may have found it easier than we do to believe that such things had actually happened.

Another difference between Old Testament belief and modern popular thought is that the latter is predominantly mechanistic in its view of the world of nature. Whereas we think of the world as a system which works in terms of 'laws', the Israelites probably had a more God-centred view of things, as seen in passages such as Psalm 104:10–24. Regularity and order in nature were perhaps for the Israelites conceived in terms of God's promises (Genesis 8:22) and his faithfulness. The differences between modern popular thought and Old Testament belief can be represented diagrammatically as on page 6.

Several points should be noted. There is no place for 'natural' and 'supernatural' in the Old Testament diagram. Though the latter has a 'miracle' pole, that concept would contain more events than would the 'miracle' pole in the popular thought diagram, for the reasons already explained. Popular thought would recognize fewer miracles, not only because the modern understanding of the regular and ordered is wider than the Old Testament understanding, but also because modern thought will apply the test of historicity to some Old Testament miracles, and will rule them out on these grounds. Thus the word 'historical' appears on the popular thought diagram (page 6), indicating that historicity plays its part in distinguishing between what may be

5

termed miracle, and what may be regarded as deriving from mere superstition or hearsay.

It is now necessary to comment on these two positions from a traditional theological perspective. The 'laws' which in popular thought are supposed to govern the natural order are, in fact, generalizations based on human observation. They do not concern the world 'as it is' (whatever that may be), but the world *as we think about it*. The way we think about it may change in the light of new knowledge, and it could

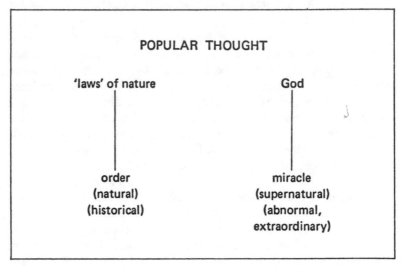

POPULAR THOUGHT

'laws' of nature   God

order   miracle
(natural)   (supernatural)
(historical)   (abnormal,
                     extraordinary)

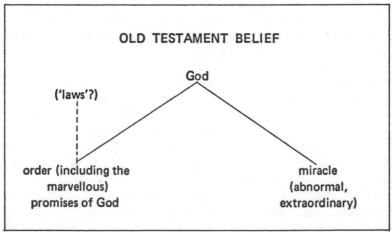

OLD TESTAMENT BELIEF

God

('laws'?)

order (including the   miracle
marvellous)   (abnormal,
promises of God   extraordinary)

6

well be that what we today regard as miraculous (that is, abnormal and extraordinary) would be regarded as ordinary by future generations. To describe order in nature in terms of 'laws' does not necessarily exclude God from the world. Indeed, like the Old Testament, the theologian may wish to claim that many regular, ordered things in nature are marvellous, and in some way reflections of God's glory (Psalm 19:1 ff). At the same time, the theologian will be careful about the way he states that God works in and through the ordered things of nature. There are many unpleasant as well as marvellous processes in the natural order ('nature red in tooth and claw') and how God is to be related to these is a concern of theology known as 'theodicy', and cannot be discussed here.[5] The problem of God's relation to the natural order is, again, a problem of *how we think* about God's relation to the world, and it is not inconsistent to affirm our belief that God *is* somehow actively related to the natural order without being able to *say adequately* how this is so. The theological position can also be represented by a diagram, in which the broken lines indicate God's relationship to the world, a relationship which, however, cannot be adequately described.

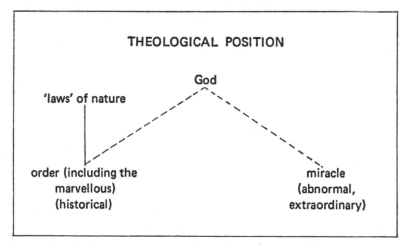

THEOLOGICAL POSITION

God

'laws' of nature

order (including the
marvellous)
(historical)

miracle
(abnormal,
extraordinary)

In this diagram, there is no real place for the natural/supernatural categories that are in the popular thought diagram, for the theologian wishes to assert, with the Old Testament, that some aspects of the ordered world are 'supernatural' in that they express the glory of God or

---

[5] See John Hick, *Evil and the God of Love*, London, 1966.

because God 'works' through them. Miracle is retained, in the sense of the abnormal or extraordinary, though much narrower in scope than for the Old Testament diagram, and the category of history is used to decide whether some alleged miracles are in fact miracles. The Resurrection of Christ is a case where the historical indications are strong (though not, in the nature of the case, conclusive) that Christ rose from death, and this event is thus a miracle in that it is certainly extraordinary and abnormal.

If we compare this diagram with the Old Testament belief diagram, we see that the two have much in common. The Old Testament scope of miracle is wider than that of the modern theologian, and the latter will use both his greater knowledge of order and regularity in nature, as well as his keener historical sense in order to remove from the category of miracle what the Old Testament might have regarded as a miracle.

To which categories will he remove these latter 'miracles'? In some cases, it will be to the category of the marvellous in the ordered world. If the plagues in Egypt were basically natural occurrences, then for the modern writer they were not miracles according to his strict definition. This is not, however, to deny that they were marvellous, for they coincided with Israel's exodus from Egypt and were seen by the Israelites as God's work on their behalf. Thus, to remove the plagues from the category of miracle does not mean that they cease to be regarded as in some sense the work of God. Where the modern writer differs from the Old Testament is merely in the scope of his category of miracle. He is at one with the Old Testament in regarding the plagues as the work of God.

In other cases, the modern writer will remove some Old Testament miracles to a category not represented on the diagrams, that of the non-historical. He may do this for several reasons. He may believe that a miracle story is an unassimilated folk-tale (see section 4). He may conclude that as a story has been passed down from one generation to another by word of mouth, the story has been progressively embellished with extraordinary or abnormal details (see also section 4). He may think that because a story comes from what I call later (in section 6) the third-hand or reported traditions of encounter between God and man, the story has utilized traditional symbols for God's presence, and is therefore not to be taken literally. By calling these traditions non-historical, it is not implied that there is no historical basis to them, but rather that it is impossible with certainty to discover their original historical character. In any case, the importance of these traditions for the theologian will not lie in whether or not they are historically true, but in the way in which they reflect Israel's belief in God. Such points will be emphasized in the expositions of the selected passages.

To conclude this section, throughout the book, the term 'super-natural' is used mainly in its popular sense of abnormal or extra-ordinary. This is a book for general readers, and the difficulties which the popular usage of 'supernatural' raises for the general reader will be tackled. The difficulties will be tackled, however, in terms of the third diagram, and the explanation which follows and precedes it.

2. MYTH

There is no doubt that the word 'myth' is offensive to some readers, because in its popular sense, it denotes something that did not happen, or which is otherwise untrue. On the whole, the word has been avoided in this book, but my treatment of some of the passages has been affected by the results of my own researches into the concept of myth as used in Old Testament studies.[6] It is, in fact, very difficult to say what myth is, and this is because the word has become a label attached to very many different things. Myths have been defined as stories about gods, as stories which accompanied rituals, as stories which were basically poetic descriptions of the workings of nature; myth has been un-derstood as a particular way of thinking about the world, different from that of modern western man. Because of this variety of definition, I think that it is best to avoid the word myth, and instead to try to identify the problems which the use of the concept of myth (however defined) has tried to solve.

My expositions of selected passages have been influenced by two ap-proaches to myth, which ought to be mentioned here. The first, which affects Genesis 3 in particular (see pages 24ff), has been advanced by the French philosopher Paul Ricoeur.[7] Ricoeur believes that myths are stories which hold together in opposition the apparent contradictory basic symbols which express man's understanding of his existence. In the Old Testament, there are expressed man's convictions that he is a free agent, rightly judged by God when God's will is disobeyed. But there is also an awareness that man is not in complete control of himself; evil is a force outside of himself, stronger than him, and to which he responds from inside of himself. Yet we feel compelled to say both that

---

[6] *Myth in Old Testament Interpretation*, W. de Gruyter, Berlin, 1974.
[7] *Philosophie de la Volonté*, Paris, 1950, II pt. 2, 'La Symbolique du Mal.'

man is fully responsible for the evil that he does, and that he is in some way forced into doing it. This is the paradox of the 'serf-arbitre', the free man who is a slave, and Ricoeur believes that in the story of Genesis 3, these apparent contradictions are held together in story form, not in order to solve the problem that the contradictions raise, for this is impossible, but in order to state at the outset of the Old Testament what the men of God in ancient Israel had learnt of their true being, as they had come to know something about God. How far Ricoeur's understanding of myth will receive any general acceptance remains to be seen, but for the present writer, it sheds a good deal of light on a narrative such as Genesis 3, and shows how the passage can be interpreted in the light of many other parts of the Old Testament.

The second discussion of myth which has influenced the approach to certain narratives in this book is that by Ernst Lohmeyer in the volume *Kerygma and Myth*.[8] This is part of a wider debate about the interpretation of the New Testament which was conducted during and after the second World War. In his essay, Lohmeyer argued,

> how else can we believe in God or speak of the gods, unless we conceive of him or them as working and having their being in this world among us men in the same mode as men speak and work? . . . It is the secret and basis (of all religion) that human conceptions, while they remain human, are nevertheless capable of apprehending the divine and so surpass all human conception.[9]

In this argument, he was trying to maintain that stories about God which describe him as encountering man in this world, in something of the way that a man encounters a man, were stories that did more than merely describe human thoughts about man's existence. Lohmeyer was maintaining that such stories were saying something about the reality beyond this world that we call God, and that it was the inadequacy of human language which necessitated the use of stories in which God was made to speak and work as men speak and work.

In the Old Testament there are a number of stories that could be described in this way, for example, Genesis chapters 18, and 32:22–32. I would want to call them 'myth' in Lohmeyer's sense, and in my expositions, I have tried to express what I think is the reality to which

[8] E. Lohmeyer, 'The Right Interpretation of the Mythological' in H. W. Bartsch (ed.), *Kerygma and Myth*, London, 1964,[2] pages 124 ff.

[9] Lohmeyer, page 126.

they point. However, I would add one further point: although these stories seem to portray God as working and speaking as men do, there is always an element of mystery in their description of the divine. This element of mystery is described further in the section 'Presence and Power' (see page 14).

3. 'ULTIMATE QUESTIONS'

Although there is no discussion later in the book of the incident in I Samuel 16:14 which speaks about the evil spirit from God which tormented Saul, the general problem which it raises is worth discussion. The obvious way of understanding the passage is as follows: the ancient Israelites had no conception of what we call depression or mental illness. Therefore, they ascribed any sort of abnormal human behaviour to God. Thus the story of Saul's evil spirit tells us nothing about God, but something about the difference between our modern understanding of things, and that of the biblical writers.

I think, however, that the matter is more complicated than this, and that when the biblical writer used the concept of the 'evil spirit from God' he was wrestling with what I call an 'ultimate question'. An ultimate question is a question of the type 'why do innocent people suffer?', 'who is ultimately responsible for evil, if not God?'. To such questions, modern philosophical theological thought can give no satisfactory *logical* answer. In the case of Saul, one strand at least of biblical tradition believed that Saul had been appointed on God's initiative (I Samuel 9:1–10:16), and that he had tried to serve his God honestly and zealously (I Samuel 28:3; II Samuel 21:2). The record was also aware of Saul's failures, and it noted his personal reasons for being jealous of David (I Samuel 18:8–9). The main difficulty for the biblical writer, however, was to explain why Saul, who had been chosen by God, had fallen from grace; why his actions had become increasingly desperate, involving murder (I Samuel 22:17–19) and the occult (I Samuel 28:8–9) before his tragic death in battle. Had God made a mistake when he chose Saul? How could the one on whom God's spirit had descended do such deeds?

These problems are similar to those with which the opening of the book of Job and I Kings 22:19–23 wrestle. Both these passages try to deal with ultimate questions, and it is significant that in both passages, something like an evil spirit appears, which has considerable freedom of action, while remaining ultimately responsible to God. I do not believe that the Old Testament, any more than modern theological thought, found the answer to these ultimate questions, but two points are worthy of consideration. Firstly, if we take the story of Saul's evil spirit from God together with Job 1–2 and I Kings 22:19–23, then the Saul story is more than merely a pre-scientific explanation of Saul's moods. It is a much deeper attempt to account for success and failure, obedience and apostasy on the part of a servant of God. Secondly, these Old Testament attempts to solve ultimate questions imply a belief in God that is far from superficial. It would be much easier, especially for ancient and less sophisticated peoples, to solve ultimate questions by believing not in one God, but in two or more opposed cosmic forces, the one (or some) evil, the other (or others) good. Belief in *one* God (and such belief is implicit throughout the Old Testament, even where the existence of other gods is not denied) puts the ultimate questions in their most acute form by creating the problem that a God who is believed to be good and to have created a good world, is ultimately responsible for evil and pain and suffering. The Old Testament writers who were bold enough to assert such a belief had not come to it by philosophical reflection, but through their openness to God, and from the conviction of ancient Israel that God had acted in decisive moments of their history, and in so doing had revealed something of his character. The ancient Israelites and the Old Testament writers may have been pre-scientific in many things, but when we are faced with narratives which appear simply to express a pre-scientific naivety, closer inspection of the text may well reveal that the real problems are philosophical and theological. I do not believe that openness to God is directly related to scientific knowledge.

4. FOLKLORE

The words 'folklore' and 'folk-tale' are likely to upset some readers just as much as the word 'myth'. All peoples seem to have their folk-tales, and it would be surprising if this had not been true for the ancient Israelites.[10] Folk-tales express some of the deepest hopes and longings of the 'ordinary' members of societies. They also often express a concern for the 'under-dog'. So you are likely to find that the stupid youngest son comes out best, or the orphan girl and not her step-mother or step-sisters is the one who marries the prince. Sometimes magical forces come to the aid of the hero or heroine, as they pass through tribulation to success.

---

[10] For a treatment of Old Testament traditions in the light of comparative folklore see T. H. Gaster, *Myth, Legend and Custom in the Old Testament,* London, 1969.

Because many of the stories recorded in books such as Genesis, Exodus, Judges and I Samuel were passed down by word of mouth for many generations they must have been influenced by the folk-tales of the ancient Israelites, but we must not necessarily assume that all such influences are bad. On the contrary, such influence probably gave to many stories in the Old Testament their dramatic shape, and helped them to express more clearly the ancient Israelite conviction that God had been active in certain events of their history.

In the section dealing with the Plagues in Egypt (page 38), I have said that I do not believe that in actual fact Moses had a series of interviews with Pharaoh, each of which was followed by a plague which Pharaoh entreated Moses to stop, only for the cycle of Pharaoh's 'obstinacy-plague-entreaty' to happen all over again. Probably, the Israelites escaped from Egypt at a time of great confusion in that country, a confusion which included a number of natural catastrophes. It was in the telling and re-telling of the story of the great deliverance that the whole complex of happenings began to assume the dramatic story form that it now has in Exodus 6–9. Moreover, because in folk-tales it is the under-dog who wins through, often assisted by magical forces, the contact between folk-tales and the telling of the story of the plagues enabled the latter better to express the underlying conviction of the Israelites that their deliverance from Egypt was an act of mercy on the part of God towards a people in need (under-dogs), accompanied by evidence of his power over nature.

There are probably four ways, at least, in which folk-tale or tales have played a part in the formation of some Old Testament passages.

(a) A passage may contain elements taken from folk-tale (for example, the talking serpent in Genesis 3).

(b) The influence of folk-tale may have shaped the story of an historical occurrence, and helped to express Israel's belief in God's action in it (for example, the traditions about the plagues in Egypt).

(c) A pure folk-tale may have been deeply assimilated into the Old Testament tradition so as to express something of the distinctive theology of the Old Testament (for example, Genesis 32:22–32 (the story of Jacob's wrestling at the river Jabbok) where several such folk-tales have probably been assimilated).

(d) A folk-tale may have entered the biblical tradition with little or no assimilation to the distinctive faith of ancient Israel (for example, the story of Gideon's fleece, Judges 6:36–46)

13

Of these four ways, only the last is probably of little value to modern readers of the Old Testament.

5. 'PRESENCE' AND 'POWER'

There seem to be some typical differences between narratives that deal with God's *presence* and those that deal with his *power*.

(*a*) Examples of the *presence* of God narratives are the visit of the three men to Abraham (Genesis 18), the call of Moses (Exodus 3:1–12) and Jacob's wrestling (Genesis 32:22 ff). A typical feature of such stories is a certain confusion between God and his messengers. Thus in Genesis 18, the three men appear to symbolize the presence of God, one of them is addressed as though he *were* God, yet God seems to speak directly to Abraham from heaven. In the incident of Jacob's wrestling, it is far from clear whether Jacob is wrestling with a man, an angel, with God, or with all of them at once! In the story of the burning bush, there is an apparent confusion between the angel who appears to Moses 'in a flame of fire out of the midst of the bush' (Exodus 3:2) and God who calls to Moses 'out of the bush'. Some of these apparent confusions may be due to the fact that the stories as they now stand are composed of several originally separate strands of tradition; but as I later note (page 35) not all of the apparent confusions can be removed by supposing that they result from the combination of different sources. While I do not claim to be able to explain satisfactorily why the apparent confusions are there if they did not result from the combination of separate sources, I believe that their presence in the narratives is not an accident.

Narratives about God's *presence* seem to be confined to traditions about what happened in Israel before Israel had a king. They are all third-hand not first-hand traditions (I shall explain the importance of this distinction shortly). It is likely that when the biblical writers came to describe the encounters with God that had taken place in the earliest times of Israelite history, they believed that God had revealed himself more directly to these men of old, compared with the way he was believed to reveal himself at the time of the biblical writers. Thus in the narratives about the encounters with God experienced by figures such as Abraham, Jacob and Moses, the biblical writers portrayed the encounters as vivid and direct meetings with the divine; yet the presence of apparent confusions in the narratives between God and his messengers helped to preserve a sense of mystery about the incidents.

(*b*) Narratives about the *power* of God are much more widely distributed throughout the Old Testament, and they constitute the bulk of what we normally regard as miracle stories. In these stories about God's power, many folk-tale elements appear which have not been assimilated into the tradition so as to express any part of the distinctive faith of the Old Testament (compare the miracles of Elisha in II Kings 4:38–44). In many of these stories, the *historical* problem of 'what really happened' is at its most acute, and although each case must be judged on its merits, it is in the area of these stories about God's power that the reader will most frequently find himself in conflict with the Old Testament text. Taken as a whole, these stories about God's power express the conviction that God is in control of the world and the happenings in it. But these stories have to be set beside the many other Old Testament passages which assert that God is working through many ordinary and non-spectacular happenings. (See section 1, *Natural and Supernatural*.)

6. THIRD-HAND AND FIRST-HAND TRADITION

Many people who read Old Testament narratives about the presence and power of God are bothered by the fact that in their day-to-day religious experience, they know of nothing comparable to what is recorded in the Old Testament. We do not see burning bushes or hear God's voice speaking audibly to us, though we may allow that very exceptionally people genuinely claim to have had such experiences. However, the Old Testament contains much that *does* match the experience of ordinary people. The Psalms, for instance, fully express the range of religious experiences familiar to modern man. God is sometimes close to the psalmist, and sometimes seems to be far off. The psalmist is filled now with faith, and now with doubt. One moment he can utter sublime praises to God, and in the next breath he can express his hatred for his enemies.

The prophetic books, too, record much about experience of God that the ordinary religious man can appreciate and they sometimes show us the ordinary 'mechanics' of how the divine message came to the prophets. The similarity of the Hebrew words for 'summer fruits' and 'end' triggered off for Amos a message about divine judgement when he saw a basket of summer fruits (Amos 8:1–3). Jeremiah received a message whilst watching a potter at work (Jeremiah 18:1–11).

These passages from the Psalms and the prophetic books represent what I have called the first-hand accounts of divine-human encounter. They are not necessarily autobiographical, but they are probably dependent on and reflect a personal tradition of encounter with God. In many

15

cases they stress the ordinariness and the indirectness of the encounter. In contrast, I describe as third-hand, or belonging to the reported tradition about encounter with God, those traditions which come especially in books such as Genesis, Exodus, Numbers and Joshua. Here, a kind of shorthand is used to describe the encounter with God, precisely because people like Moses were too far removed in time from the writers of the Old Testament for a first-hand tradition to go back to them. We shall never know the exact nature of the experience of God in the life of Moses. This means that especially in the opening books of the Old Testament, phrases such as 'The Lord said unto Moses' are not to be taken literally, as though Moses actually heard a voice. We can assume that this is shorthand, expressing the Old Testament conviction that Moses did in some way receive divine communications, though it would be reasonable to suppose that in fact his experience was not essentially different from that described in what I call the first-hand tradition.

It is to be acknowledged that this distinction is a rough and ready one, and that it leaves much unsaid. For example, in Amos 7:8 we have the phrase 'The Lord said unto me', and it is well known that narratives such as the call of Moses (Exodus 3) were influenced by the pattern assumed by first-hand accounts of calls to prophets (for example, by Isaiah 6 and Jeremiah 1). Moreover, even a first-hand account of religious experience tends to be expressed in certain typical or traditional phrases (compare testimonies of religious conversion), and this is true of the first-hand tradition in the Old Testament. Whatever the inadequacies of my first-hand/third-hand or reported distinction, I believe that it will help the reader to understand some of the Old Testament narratives where encounter with God is described in terms quite outside his ordinary experience, and I believe that the distinction can be to some extent tested out in one of the practical activities for individual or group use, at the end of the book.

7. SOURCES AND TRADITIONS

Old Testament scholars have believed for many generations that some books of the Old Testament, especially books like Genesis and Exodus, reached their present form when an editor or editors wove together what were originally separate written sources. The earliest *observations* along these lines go back at least 1,000 years! The reader who has not met this view before is recommended to read Genesis 6:5–9:17 in the Authorised, Revised or Revised Standard Version, or the New English Bible. It is easy to discern large blocks of material in which either the name 'God' appears, or in which the divine name is 'the Lord' (6:5–8, 7:1–5, 8:6–12, though there is no divine name in the last reference, 8:20–22 for 'the Lord' passages; 6:9–22, 7:7–23 although 'the Lord' occurs in verse 16, 8:1–5, 13–19, 9:1–17, for 'God' passages). These blocks of material represent two originally separate written accounts of the Flood.

In my explanations of passages, I have insisted strongly that it is the narrative *as it now stands* which must be interpreted, and not what scholars suggest about a narrative's possible earlier stages. However, I have often referred to sources and traditions that possibly underlie the narratives, in order to help the reader to see why there is unevenness in some passages, and why some elements seem not to fit the main theme of the story. Where I speak of the Yahwist source, I refer to a collection of traditions written down probably in the 10th or 9th century BC. Where I speak of the Priestly source, I mean a collection of traditions probably written down in the 6th or 5th century BC. The dates suggested for the time of writing down of the sources do not imply that everything to be found in a source had no existence in any form before the written compilation was made; nor do I exclude the possibility that when the written compilations were made, they incorporated *already-written* material. By traditions, as opposed to sources, I mean the smaller units which were gathered together into the two main written sources.

8. MIRACLES AND HISTORICITY

The philosophical and definition problems of miracles have been mentioned in the first section of this introduction (pages 3ff). Here, I propose to outline the question at the historical level: how do we decide which miracles happened?

Where we have a group of miracle stories, as in the Elijah/Elisha cycles, in which the miracles performed can be paralleled from miracles related in other folk literatures, it is likely that those similar Old Testament miracles attributed to Elijah and Elisha did not happen. We have already noted that in the Elijah/Elisha cycles, we have our largest body of unassimilated folk-tales in the Old Testament (see page 15), and as in other folk literatures, the miraculous element in the stories has been produced by the exaggerations that occur as the stories are told and re-told. However, I do not believe that every miracle in the Elijah/Elisha cycles is to be explained in this way. Some of the miracle stories in this part of the Old Testament are self-contained, or merely tacked on to the

17

end of another narrative, while other miracle stories are vital to a quite complicated piece of narrative. The extent to which a narrative is embedded in its context is an important factor when we come to try to interpret it. Thus, there is a lot of difference between many of the Elijah/Elisha stories and the incidents of the drought and the fire from heaven (I Kings 17–18). These last two incidents are closely connected together, and they do not just involve groups of the disciples of the prophets, but concern the Israelite king and nation. Thus, in my exposition of this passage, I shall treat it differently from many of the other miracle stories.

Another way in which miracle stories have come into being in the Old Testament is by the operation of the third-hand process. As writers tried to describe how God disclosed himself to his people in the ancient times of Abraham, Jacob and Moses, they heightened the wonder element precisely because they used their third-hand shorthand language about the encounter, and its mystery.

Miracle stories, then, must be assessed according to their literary type and aim, and their relation to the context in which they occur. The clues provided by such assessments will help us in our historical exercise of trying to reconstruct 'what really happened'.

Ultimately, I would want to go most of the way with the view of miracles and the supernatural in the Old Testament, expressed by one of the greatest Old Testament scholars of our generation, the late Professor H. H. Rowley:

> If miracle be defined as divine activity within the world, a belief in its possibility would seem to be fundamental to a belief in God. He cannot be excluded from the world he has made, or reduced to the position of a spectator of the interplay of forces which he had once set in motion. In the faith of Israel he was too real and personal to be reduced to impotence in his own world, or regarded as one who idly watched while men worked out their own destiny, and this faith is integral to any worth-while faith in God. Many of the miracles recorded in the Old Testament are examples of divine activity through natural events, such as the deliverance from Egypt through wind and wave, from Sisera through storm, or from Sennacherib through plague. Others are examples of divine activity through events which were contrary to the order of nature, such as the passage through walls of water at the Red Sea, the standing still of the sun in the time of Joshua, the recovery of an axe head by Elisha by the device of throwing wood into the water, or the delivery of the three youths from Nebuchadnezzar's fire. In some cases these stories are dramatic representations of simpler facts, as may be seen by a study of the context in which

they are set; or wonder tales that grew round the name of a hero; or parabolic stories that were made the vehicle of a message. The miracle stories can neither be uncritically accepted as historical, nor uncritically rejected as fancy. Each example must be examined for itself, in the light of the character of the narrative in which it stands and the purpose for which it appears to have been written. But that there is a truly miraculous element in the story I am fully persuaded. We have not merely the working out of human impulses and the chance interplay of natural forces. We have the activity of God in inspiration and revelation, and the evidence of his presence in Nature and history.[1]

---

[1] H. H. Rowley, *The Faith of Israel*, SCM, London, 1956, pages 58–59.

II SELECT PASSAGES

1

THE CREATION

Genesis 1:1–2:4a

Two major difficulties are probably felt by modern readers of the first chapter of the Bible. The first is how to reconcile the biblical account of creation with scientific theories; the second arises because many commentaries compare Genesis 1 with creation stories from Israel's neighbours in the ancient Near East.

Although the majority of professional theologians and biblical scholars have long since ceased to be bothered by the reconciling of Genesis 1 with scientific theories, the same is not true for many ordinary readers. 'God versus science' still arouses great interest. In 1972, the BBC Radio Four service devoted some two hours to an evening programme on the subject, and from time to time, new scientific theories such as the 'big bang' theory of creation arouse interest among those who look for scientific confirmation of the Bible.

In dealing with the problem, it will be difficult to do other than repeat well-known arguments. First, scientific method is concerned, among other things, with generalization and attempted explanation. It observes phenomena, and tries to make generalizations or hypotheses about them. In the nature of the case, such explanations or hypotheses cannot be *proved*, they can only be *falsified* or be found to be *inadequate*. When this happens, new hypotheses are framed, and these form the basis of scientific explanation until such time as *they* are found to be inadequate in the light of new knowledge or experimentation. Thus there is no finality, especially in such a matter as the origin of the universe. Science involves a continuous discovery of facts, and a continuous framing of hypotheses to account for them.

Genesis 1 undoubtedly contains an element of Hebrew science. Not only has it long been known that in the picture of the world implied in the opening verses—a flat earth enclosed by a semi-spherical dome (the firmament) above which were waters (the waters above the firmament) etc—the Hebrews shared a scientific outlook with other peoples of the ancient Near East, but recent suggestions by anthropologists have shed more light on the scientific outlook underlying the account. It has been suggested that Genesis 1, with its distinctions between light and darkness, water and earth, above the firmament and below the firmament, and so on, displays the sort of classification in terms of opposites that characterizes the perception of the world by 'primitive' peoples as well as modern scientific classification. According to this suggestion, man, however primitive or sophisticated, can only order the mass of sense impressions that come in upon him by dividing them, in terms of opposites, into larger and smaller classes of things that have certain features in common. Thus in Genesis 1, the earth is distinguished from the seas, and the earth-creatures from the sea-creatures; but within earth, trees and plants which are self-propagating are distinguished from the animals which must mate in order to reproduce. This suggestion, then, tells us a lot about why many of the details in Genesis 1 are presented in the way that they are.

If Genesis 1 *contains* 'science', it follows that this science can be no more final than any other science. Just as the scientific explanations of the 1970's have superseded those of the 1870's, and will in turn themselves be superseded by those of the 2070's, so those of Genesis 1 will never now be anything more than evidence for what people thought about the scientific nature of the world nearly 3000 years ago. But this is not to say that Genesis 1 is therefore devoid of all value. It is often said that science can only deal with the 'how' of things and not the 'why'—which is a popular way of saying that theological statements (and most of Genesis 1 is theology) are different from scientific statements. Thus it has been repeatedly asserted that the science of Genesis 1 is not important. What matters is what the narrative has to say about God's relation to the world.

At this point, however, we meet the second difficulty mentioned at the outset of this section. For almost as long as commentators have asserted that the theology implied in Genesis 1 is not in conflict with scientific theories, they have also asserted that Genesis 1 is a Hebrew version of a story about the creation of the world that was well known in the ancient Near East. The basis of this theory was the discovery, in the 1870's, of the Babylonian account of creation (although some features of this Babylonian account had been known, for example, from 4th century AD reports of Eusebius of Caesarea). Although it has been illuminating to read expositions of Genesis 1 in the light of other accounts of creation from the ancient Near East, it is also arguable that such expositions have done less justice to wider theological questions because attention has been focused on how the belief of ancient Israel differed from that of her neighbours. The ordinary reader has been given treatments of Genesis 1 which described the *distinctive features* of the Hebrew as against the other accounts of creation, but he has not necessarily been told how Genesis 1 can teach him something about God in spite of its antiquated science.

All new discoveries tend to influence scholarly theory more than the evidence warrants, and later generations of scholars then correct the balance. In the case of Genesis 1, there appears to be a growing tide of opinion against regarding it merely as a Hebrew version of an ancient popular creation story. If many scholars do not go so far as to make such a denial, they are at least ready to allow that Genesis 1 should be interpreted more in terms of its own structure and ideas than in contrast to its ancient Near Eastern background. The case for the denial of a connexion between Genesis 1 and the Babylonian story is briefly as follows. The Babylonian version consists of two main elements—first, the story of a battle between the gods, and second, the creation of the world by the victorious god, Marduk. Clearly, Genesis 1 has nothing corresponding to the first main element, and it is not absolutely clear that the parallels between Genesis 1 and the second element demonstrate a connexion. (The cases are clearly set out and discussed in A. Heidel, *The Babylonian Genesis,* Chicago, 1951.) However, it has been argued that *traces* of the first element, that a battle between the gods, can be found in Old Testament passages such as Psalm 89:10 and Isaiah 51:9–10 where God's defeat of powers of chaos are mentioned, thus proving that both elements of the Babylonian story were known to the ancient Hebrews, although the first element was not *directly* used in Genesis 1, apart from possible echoes of it in Genesis 1:2.

Against this, it has been maintained that the Babylonian story is untypical of the literature of the period in combining the two elements. There are creation stories from the ancient Near East which contain no account of a battle between gods, while there are accounts of battles between gods which do not lead on to creation. Thus there is no firm evidence that Genesis 1 is connected with any story in which the creation is preceded by a battle between gods. Further, the chapter itself shows signs of the combination of several different, and perhaps originally separate, elements.

First, and best known, is the six-day scheme into which the creative acts have been placed. But there are not six, but eight creative acts, necessitating that two acts of creation take place on the third and sixth days. Moreover, there are ten instances of the phrase 'God said' (verses 3, 6, 9, 11, 14, 20, 24, 26, 28, 29). It has also been noticed that in addition to the verb 'created', the verb 'made' is found in the chapter (for example, verses 7, 16, 25) and an original strand characterized by this latter verb has been surmised. It looks, then, as though it is too simple to regard Genesis 1 as a Hebraized version of the Babylonian story. Whatever the connexions, if any, the chapter gives indications of its own long process of composition, in which the end product has not obliterated traces of various originally separate strands or ideas.

This makes us look to the chapter itself for clues to its theological significance. Two words in particular have received attention. The verb translated 'created' (Hebrew: *bara*) is used in the Old Testament only of God's creative activity, and although some commentators have made too much of this fact, it can safely be concluded that the use of *bara* indicates that the creative process, where God is concerned, is unlike any other creative process. Already, then, the biblical text is stating in its own way what modern theology would say differently, that statements about God's activity are not the same sort of statements as those concerning processes within the natural universe.

If *bara* has important theological connotations, it is the more so true of the verb 'said' in the phrases 'God said'. The model of creation by means of the spoken word (which is not in itself unique to the ancient Israelites) not only asserts a relation between the Creator and creation, but leaves the exact nature of the relation sufficiently unspecified to allow the transcendence of God to be maintained. The notion of the 'word of God' in the whole of the Old Testament has also to be taken into account. According to the Old Testament, God discloses his will to his servants the prophets by means of his word, and the great crises of ancient Israel's history have been foreknown and faced through prophetic reception and proclamation of the word. God has revealed his will to his people in the ten words (Deuteronomy 4:13 see RV margin) or commandments of Mount Sinai, which detail a man's duties to God and his neighbour.

Genesis 1 is thus asserting the dependence of the created order on the God who has made himself known to Israel through the prophetic interpretation of significant events in the life of the people. Because this God is a God who speaks his word to his people through prophet and priest, and who calls Israel to loyalty to himself as a person, the God whose word brings the created order into being is no abstraction or first cause, but one who makes moral and personal demands, in obedience to which alone the true nature of the Creator and the creation can be understood.

These, then, are the lines along which the teaching of Genesis 1 is to be sought. Not as opposed to modern science, nor in distinction to other ancient Near Eastern texts is it best understood, but in terms of its own structures and key words, and against the general background of Old Testament belief. Genesis 1 stands or falls with the rest of the Old Testament and cannot be isolated from it.

Several points of translation and interpretation call for comment:

Does Genesis 1 imply *creatio ex nihilo* (creation out of nothing)? Since the fourth Lateran Council of 1215, *creatio ex nihilo* has been an article of the Christian faith, although it is not explicitly mentioned in the Apostles' and Nicene creeds. If the doctrine is supposed to mean that God did not create the world out of any pre-existent matter, it has to be said that this problem probably did not occur to the Hebrews in this way. If, however, the doctrine asserts the uniqueness of God, and the *dependence* of the created order in some sense on him, then this can be supported from Genesis 1.

An allied question concerns the translation of Genesis 1 : 1. It has long been argued that this should be translated 'When God began to create the heavens and the earth (now the earth was waste and void . . . upon the face of the waters) God said: Let there be light', although the New English Bible is the first 'authorized' version to put something like this down as the main text. Such renderings have often been justified by referring to the Babylonian account, where the world is created from the carcass of the defeated goddess Tiamat, of whom an echo has often been detected in the Hebrew word translated 'waste' (verse 2). Also, there has sometimes been an over-reaction against the more traditional rendering because of the way in which it has been made to support the doctrine of *creatio ex nihilo*.

Although the traditional translation is not free from difficulty, I do not believe that Genesis 1 began with such a complicated sentence as the New English Bible rendering implies. The opening 'In the beginning God created the heaven and the earth' is probably a summary of all that follows. The passage then goes on to describe the formless matter out of which an ordered universe was created. The question whether God also created the formless matter, or how it had otherwise got there, probably did not bother the Hebrew writers. The New English Bible translates the phrase 'spirit of God' of verse 2 as 'a mighty wind'. Again, although this translation is theoretically possible, I do not think that this is what the Hebrew phrase conveyed to the ancient Israelites. If the traditional translation is correct, the passage indicates that divine influence was not absent from the formless matter which was to be the basis of the creation. The whole creation is thus from the beginning 'good' (verse 4 etc) and we are reminded that the account is more concerned with the moral character of the creation dependent upon a holy God, than with speculation about the origin of matter out of which the universe may or may not have been formed.

It goes without saying that scientific theory makes no attempt to comment on the moral character of the universe. To detached observation, the universe is both good and bad, both wonderful and barbaric. Only in commitment to the God who speaks through his word in its various forms, can one have faith in the moral character and purpose of the creation, and Genesis 1 takes this commitment for granted.

2

THE FALL

Genesis 2:4b–3:24

The story of the Garden of Eden and the 'fall' has, like Genesis 1, been compared with traditions from outside the Bible; but it, too, shows signs of being composed of several originally separate strands of tradition, and it must be interpreted in terms of its own final structure. Probably the closest parallel to our passage from outside the Bible is the incident in the *Epic of Gilgamesh*[1] where a serpent deprives Gilgamesh of the plant which bestows immortality. In the *Myth of Adapa*[2], the hero on good advice, refuses bread and water, only to be told that he has lost immortality by his refusal. On a famous Babylonian seal[3] (which is a

---

[1] The *Epic of Gilgamesh* is a text that was widely known in the ancient Near East, parts of which date from at least 1500 BC. The *Epic* is known to us mainly from texts found in the library of Ashurbanipal (669–627) at Nineveh. For translations of the Epic see A. Heidel, *The Gilgamesh Epic and Old Testament Parallels*, Chicago, 1949 and J. B. Pritchard (ed.), *Ancient Near Eastern Texts*, Princeton, 1955, pages 237 ff.

[2] *The Myth of Adapa* was also widely known in the ancient Near East, and fragments of the text were found at El Amarna (Egypt—14th century BC) and the library of Ashurbanipal. See *Ancient Near Eastern Texts*, pages 101 ff.

[3] The seal is reproduced, for example, in J. B. Pritchard (ed.), *Ancient Near East in Pictures*, Princeton, 1969.

hazardous parallel since it has no accompanying text) is portrayed a tree with fruit upon it, two clothed figures, male and female, sitting upon stools, with hands outstretched towards the fruit, and a serpent erect upon its tail.

In the biblical story, the following separate themes can be discerned:

(a) there is a pun on the Hebrew words for Adam and earth (Adam—Hebrew *'ādām,* earth—Hebrew *'adāmāh,* Genesis 2:7, 3:19). This suggests that there was originally a separate story explaining why, among the ancient Hebrews, man had to till the ground in order to live, and why he was buried in the ground when he died.

(b) the story of the creation of woman, with more Hebrew word-play (*'īsh* (=man)—*'ishshāh* (=out of man), compare 2:23) and a link with the verse (2:24) which explains the marriage institution.

(c) various other explanations: why serpents go on their bellies (3:14), why humans wear clothes (3:7, 21), why husbandry is hard work (3:17–19) and why childbirth is painful (3:16).

(d) many commentators hold that the material about the tree of life was originally a separate unit because apart from its mention in 2:9 and 3:22–24, it plays no part in the story.

It is not the place here to discuss in what manner these possible originally separate elements were woven together to give us the story as we now have it. Although many commentaries and monographs have attempted to do this, no large measure of agreement has been reached, and, in any case, attempts to interpret hypothetical original forms of the story divert attention away from the text as it stands.

The general reader will probably be less interested in the literary history of Genesis 2–3, and more concerned with the following questions: were Adam and Eve historical persons? did the Hebrews believe that the serpent actually spoke? how did the eating of the fruit affect Adam and Eve—was it the act of disobedience in eating the fruit or something about the fruit itself which 'opened their eyes'?

A few Christians may feel that they must believe that Adam and Eve were real persons because St Paul apparently believed so, and based his doctrine of sin, death, redemption, and the contrast between Adam and Christ on this belief (Romans 5:12–17). But should New Testament opinions about the Old Testament determine the interpretation of the Old Testament? Most Old Testament scholars would say no; and most New Testament scholars would say that we can accept what St. Paul is saying here, without accepting his views on Adam and Eve. In Romans

5:12–17, St Paul was trying essentially to say two things: first, that although sin was not reckoned until the law was given by Moses, sin and death were nevertheless present in the world *before* the giving of the law; second, that as Adam symbolizes a humanity that is characterized by sin and death, Christ sets men free from both. St Paul's first point was a problem of concern to 1st century Jews, and could only be conducted by means of the sort of arguments likely to be convincing to Jews at that time. It is not a problem likely to worry readers of this book. St Paul's second point will surely be accepted by Christians whatever their views about Adam and Eve.

What makes it impossible for most modern readers to accept the historicity of Adam and Eve is the fact that we know that earliest man was a hunter and food gatherer rather than the settled agriculturalist that Adam was, according to Genesis 2–3. Also, although monogenism (the theory that the human race originated from one group or pair of humans in one part of the world) cannot be entirely discarded, experts tend more towards the view that the human race 'emerged' from more than one centre of the world.[4] Had St Paul lived at a time when he knew these facts, he would no doubt have conducted his argument differently, but it is certain that his basic assertions would have been unaltered. He would have proclaimed that all mankind is subject to sin and death, and that Christ sets men free from both. The same is true of the doctrine of 'original sin'. What is important about the doctrine is not *how* a tendency to do evil is transmitted from generation to generation, but *that* each generation is prone to sin. It has to be noted further, however, and this is of great importance, that to say that mankind is prone to sin is not to make an assertion merely based on general observation. 'Sin' is a *theological* word, and we can only truly learn what sin is by drawing closer to God. Sin itself can dull our awareness of it. The writer, or final editor of Genesis 2–3, had this in common with St Paul and the framers of the doctrine of original sin, that his description of the human condition derived from his experience of closeness to God and not only from general observation. It expressed his understanding of himself in the light of his closeness to God and it summed up a similar awareness within the Israelite community.

The answer to the question whether the ancient Israelites believed that the serpent actually spoke is usually 'yes'. It is often said that the Israelites, like primitive peoples, would have no difficulty in believing in

---

[4] A popular treatment of this particular problem is to be found in the UNESCO magazine *Courier*, August–September 1972.

a beginning time when animals spoke. The same question arises with regard to Balaam's ass (Numbers 22:21–35), Jotham's fable (Judges 9:7–15) and the fable of Jehoash (II Kings 14:9–10). In the case of the two fables, the Israelites were probably well able to appreciate that trees and plants do not normally speak, and that the fables were stories, and not meant as serious history. I think that we should also allow that many, if not most Israelites did not take the speaking animals of Genesis 3 and Numbers 22 as serious history either, and that they regarded the point of the stories as lying elsewhere than in their historicity.

For the origin of the talking serpent and the forbidden fruit we must probably look, as has long been recognized, to folk-tales. Many stories about serpents and magic fruits are found in folk-tales the world over, and it is in folklore that animals speak.

It is also folklore which provides the answer to the question whether the fruit itself or the act of disobedience 'opened the eyes' of Adam and Eve. It was probably the magical effects of the fruit itself which 'opened their eyes', although of course the fruit could not have been eaten without the act of disobedience. Granted that the writer or final editor combined folk-tale elements about a serpent and a forbidden fruit with the other elements mentioned earlier, what does the whole story mean? In its present form it has, from start to finish, a dramatic structure which makes it a whole. Although the tree of life may have come from an originally separate unit, it is necessary for the conclusion of the story—the driving of Adam and Eve from Eden (3:22–24). Again, although many scholars argue that 3:14–19 was originally a separate unit, 3:19 makes sense only in the light of 2:7 and 3:23.

I have already outlined my understanding of Genesis 3 in the Introduction (page 9). It explains many features of ordinary life—marriage, childbirth, work—but it also says something about the human condition as understood through ancient Israel's encounter with God. Through that encounter, Israel had learned that God was just, merciful and holy. Man was unfaithful to God and unjust to his neighbour, and God's judgements were consequently deserved. Yet evil, while not residing in God, was a force both outside of man, and within him. Although in one sense man was free and therefore responsible for his wrongdoings, in other ways he was a prisoner in the power of evil, while still recognizing the justice of God's judgements against human wrongdoing.

In Genesis 2–3, these apparent contradictions are not given a philosophical solution, for such a solution is impossible; rather, they are brought and held together. The serpent is described as one of the creatures which God made (Genesis 3:1), so that there is no suggestion that there is a power of evil which from the beginning was independent of God. Yet at the same time, the serpent does symbolize a power of evil outside of man—a power of evil which seeks to be allied with man's inner desires for self-advancement. In 3:6 the psychology of temptation is described in masterly fashion:

> when the woman saw that the tree was good for food, and that it was a delight to the eyes, and that the tree was to be desired to make one wise, she took of its fuit and ate.

3:8 expresses the sense of alienation from God which sin entails, while in 3:10–13 Adam and Eve try to avoid responsibility for their disobedience.

It is often said that apart from a possible connexion with Ezekiel 28:11 ff., Genesis 3 is never referred to in the rest of the Old Testament, and the conclusion is thus often drawn that the ancient Israelites did not know, or paid little heed to, the teaching that modern interpreters believe it to possess. However, it is unlikely that a story which came to be put in such a significant position in the Old Testament can have had no importance in ancient Israel. Indeed, much that we find in the Psalms and the prophets about the human condition expresses the same apparent contradictions that are held together in Genesis 3; for example, Psalm 51:3–5, and the prophetic description of sinful Israel as a faithless wife.

Genesis 3 expresses a view of the human condition which is not primarily based on general observation of human behaviour, but which springs from the insights afforded by the closeness to God of the men of the Old Testament. That is why no adequate theology can avoid coming to grips with this passage.

3

ABRAHAM'S THREE VISITORS

Genesis 18

Genesis 18 is a narrative about the *presence* of God. It is characterized by a 'confusion' between the three men who visit Abraham, and God who speaks to Abraham directly. It is tempting to explain the difficulties by assuming that our present narrative is composed of several originally separate units, in one of which God spoke directly to Abraham, in another of which a divine messenger dealt with Abraham, and in a third of which Abraham welcomed three guests. But on the whole, critics have not tried to solve the difficulties in this way.

One recent commentator has described the relation between the three men and God as 'problematical'. 18:1 begins by saying that God appeared to Abraham by the oaks of Mamre. In verse 2, on lifting up his eyes, Abraham saw three men, and although he recognized them as important, he did not regard any one of them as divine. In verse 3 (see the detailed discussion later) Abraham addresses a singular 'my lord', presumably directing his speech to the leader of the group. In verses 5 and 9, the three men speak, but in verse 10 we return abruptly to the singular. In verse 13 God explicitly speaks, but in verse 16 the men leave Abraham on their way to Sodom, after which God enters into dialogue with Abraham. Verse 21 makes God say 'I will go down and see . . .' as though he has been absent from the scene hitherto, a point clearly contradicted earlier, for example in verse 10.

Some interpretations have tried to smooth out the difficulty in verse 3, where Abraham addresses a 'my lord' by altering the Hebrew vowels so as to read 'my lords' (so NEB '"Sirs" he said, "if I have deserved your favour . . ."'). This is quite possible, but does not remove the other difficulties.

The relation between the three men and God has been explained in two main ways. First, that one of them was God, the one who spoke in verse 10, and the other two were the angels who went on to Sodom and Gomorrah in Chapter 19. The second is that God was somehow present in all three men (this interpretation does not commit us to seeing a prefiguring of the Trinity although many early Christian commentators did argue this). The second suggestion is more likely to be correct, as it is doubtful whether the writer would have wanted to be so crude as to suggest that God himself visited Abraham in the guise of a traveller.

The exact relation between the travellers and God is, however, less important than the fact that whether deliberately or not, the confusion in the narrative expresses the transcendence and immanence of God. The three men symbolize the presence of God, but only obscurely. God remains in heaven yet he is active in the affairs of men, and concerned with matters such as the disappointments of an elderly childless couple. He speaks his word of promise, and his message is received, even if it is hard to believe. This narrative tries to draw aside a veil to permit us to see something of the mystery of what is for many a daily miracle—that of hearing and obeying God's word.

4

THE SACRIFICE OF ISAAC

Genesis 22:1–19

The questions about this passage which have worried both general readers and commentators have been moral questions. Does God put people to the test in the way that Abraham was tested? Would God command a person to sacrifice his own son? On the whole, commentators have answered both these questions by 'no', and have then tried to explain why it is that the Old Testament itself implies the answer 'yes' to both questions! A common argument has been that a story such as the offering of Isaac could only have arisen and been accepted among a people where the rights of the individual were not fully recognized, and where child sacrifice was practised or known to be practised. It has been maintained that the story marks the point in ancient Israel's history when it was realized that God did not want human sacrifice. Another view has interpreted the story as a cult legend preserved at a sanctuary, and explaining why animal offerings had been substituted for child offerings.

It is not the intention of the comments that follow to deny the impressive evidence set out in the commentaries that human sacrifice was practised in the ancient Near East, and even in ancient Israel. It is also possible either that the story marks a general protest in Israel against child sacrifice, or that it originated in a similar sense at a particular cult centre. The main question is from what angle should the story as it now stands be approached? In its present form the text says nothing about child sacrifice in ancient Israel.

If we try to imagine what must have been the mental attitude of Abraham himself (and the narrative is notably silent about this, in contrast to the portrayal of the psychology of the disobedience of Adam and Eve) we are faced squarely with the question of what could have led Abraham to believe that God was asking him to sacrifice another human being. But this is not the only possible starting-point. From Abraham's point of view, the fact that Isaac would live was not known; but for readers, both ancient and modern, the case is different. We *know* the

32

outcome of the story before we read it; we know that God does not really want the life of Isaac, but rather wishes to test Abraham's obedience, and this fact makes all the difference to the way we view the divine command to Abraham. Further, Isaac is not just anybody, and any child would have sufficed if the story were merely about the ending of child sacrifice. Isaac is the means whereby the divine promises to Abraham will be fulfilled, and God's plan for mankind will be accomplished. Thus what is amazing about God's command to Abraham is not that Abraham is directed to kill a child, but that God commands something which threatens to destroy the divine plan for the blessing of mankind through Abraham's descendants. In this way, the narrative expresses God's absolute sovereignty and freedom. If he chooses, he can appear to destroy plans which he seems to have made.

If we are to try to understand the passage in psychological or experiential terms, then we must not try to imagine what Abraham might have thought God was commanding him to do; we must look to the experience of the writer, and of Israel. The Israelites had come to know God as someone good, but unsafe. God could seem far off, he could act as though to destroy his people and annul his promises, yet always his plan was later made clear. The story of the offering of Isaac expresses the fact that the man of faith and the divine community will pass through periods when God's plan seems to be in danger of failure. After the story had been written in its present form, Israel experienced the traumas of the destruction of Jerusalem and the exile to Babylon, and Jeremiah accused God of having deceived him (Jeremiah 20:7). And yet God's purposes had not been frustrated or brought to nothing, and those who continued in obedience in times of great uncertainty often—but not always—saw the answer to their uncertainty.

The modern reader is most unlikely to come to feel that God is commanding him to destroy part of the Christian scheme of salvation. He may, however, be asked to do things that disturb his secue pattern of church life. These may involve giving up familiar buildings and forms of worship, or demand close co-operation with those whose doctrine he distrusts. He may then feel that his view of the divine plan is under attack, and although he should not be passive and uncritical, he should also ponder Genesis 22. The quality of obedience and courage symbolized in the story of Abraham and Isaac will be needed at some time by all those who follow the God of Abraham.

JACOB AT JABBOK

Genesis 32:22–32

It is fascinating to live in an old house, which has been altered from time to time over the years. You may be able to discover that the present dining room was formerly the kitchen, and that the present kitchen was built on to the house some time later, and that there was once a toilet in the basement. Interesting as it is to try to reconstruct the past history of the house, it is the present house in which you have to live.

Genesis 32:22–32 has been likened to an old house which was added to and altered over the years. Among parts of the basic material can be discerned:

(a) a pun on the name of the river 'Jabbok' (verse 22) (Hebrew *yabbok*) and the verb 'wrestled' (verse 24) (Hebrew *yēābēk*)—evidently, according to one story, the river was called Jabbok because of the wrestling

(b) an explanation of why the Israelites do not eat the sinew of the hip (verses 25, 31–32)

(c) an explanation of why the sanctuary at Penuel was so named (verse 30)

(d) an explanation of the name 'Israel' and an account of why Jacob also bore this name (verse 28; see 35:10 for another bestowal of the name 'Israel' upon Jacob)

(e) the motif of a river spirit trying to prevent a traveller from crossing.

Because, continuing the analogy of the old house, the original features and purposes of parts of a house can only be guessed from its present structure if we do not possess original plans, there are different opinions about the origin of our passage. Some have compared it with the sort of folk-tale in which spirits have to return to their world before daybreak (compare verse 26). Some have suggested a connexion with a limping ritual dance enacted at Penuel. Others have suggested that the narrative records Israel's conquest of the sanctuary at Penuel, and the incorporation of the worship of its god into the religion of Israel. Others, again, have suggested that the original combatants in the story were Jacob and Esau.

In view of the long and complex evolution of the passage to its present form, it is clearly dangerous to try to explain away its strange elements by saying, for example, that it was a dream dreamed by Jacob on the eve of the crisis of his encounter with Esau (chapter 33). Also, the lack of unanimity among scholars about the original form and meaning of the story should make us cautious about adding to the number of suggestions.

The first thing that can be said about the passage is that like Genesis 18 it concerns the *presence* of God, and that like Genesis 18 it expresses the divine presence in a deliberately confusing way. Thus, just as Abraham did not regard the three visitors as themselves divine, so here, Jacob wrestles with a man, but does not seem to realize that he is more than a man until the latter disables Jacob's thigh by supernatural means. Again, the mystery of the divine presence is retained in that the man refuses to tell Jacob his name, although he has declared that Jacob has prevailed in his wrestling with *God* (verse 28).

It is possible to interpret the story:

(*a*) in terms of the character of Jacob. Verse 28 'thy name shall be no more called Jacob' recalls the bad associations of the name 'Jacob', such as 'supplanter' (Genesis 25:26 RV margin), and reminds us of Jacob's treachery towards his brother Esau, and of his astuteness with his father-in-law Laban. Jacob's encounter with God results in a new character as well as a new name.

(*b*) in terms of the experience of encounter with God on the part of the editor(s). It can be argued that it was the unpleasant, self-seeking side of Jacob's personality (Genesis 28:20–22) which made him persist in his wrestling. The result was that Jacob's energies were brought more fully into line with God's will, but not without cost to Jacob, as seen in the pain in his thigh, and his subsequent disability (verses 25, 31). Also, the result of Jacob's striving was that his knowledge of God became deeper and more personal (verse 30). By so portraying Jacob, the editor has possibly expressed his understanding of experience of God: that the energies that can make the character of a person unattractive can be put to God's service, that this involves pain, but that a deeper relationship with God results.

Can these suggestions in the last two paragraphs be legitimately derived from the text? In one sense, they can no more be objectively supported than can the various suggestions about the original form of the story. Also, like these latter suggestions, their plausibility to each reader depends on the reader's presuppositions. Those who regard Genesis as a collection of primitive stories put together by editors whose moral and religious outlook was far inferior to theirs will presumably be reluctant to go as far as does the exposition here. However, if we allow for some sophistication and genuine experience of God on the part of the editor(s), we may accept that an old, much re-shaped story of probably non-Israelite origin has been used to express the Israelite experience of the mystery of encounter with God, its transforming effect, and its cost to the person involved.

6

THE BURNING BUSH

Exodus 3:1–6

Commentators are generally agreed that the incident of the burning bush originally existed in two separate sources, which have been combined here. Thus, for example, in verse 4, the abrupt change of divine name from 'the Lord' to 'God' can be attributed to the fact that one source usually employed the divine name 'the Lord', while the other used the name 'God' (See Introduction, page 17). However, it has also been accepted that even within the source using 'the Lord', there is an apparent confusion between 'the Lord' and the 'angel of the Lord'. Thus in verse 2 it is the angel who appears and causes the bush to burn, whereas in verse 4 it was presumably 'the Lord' who spoke directly to Moses. The combination of two sources is not itself responsible, then, for the sort of apparent confusion between God and his messengers which we have argued to be characteristic of stories about the *presence* of God. This confusion is found in one of the sources, and its function is to emphasize that while the divine presence is a mystery, yet it was this presence that Moses encountered.

When we turn to consider the burning bush itself, the question asked by most readers is 'what happened?' Conservative commentators have regarded the burning bush as something seen by Moses himself. The fact that it was burning has been explained in terms of a sunset, or as resulting from the full bloom of a bush known as 'burning bush', but such natural explanations have been regarded as less important than the fact that God somehow attracted the attention of Moses to a particular spot, and there spoke his word to Moses.

An explanation in terms of natural phenomena has also been favoured by commentators who are not conservative. They have not supposed that Moses himself saw anythir: (at least one such commentator has even denied the historical existence of Moses), but have pointed to stories about burning bushes told among other peoples. They have argued that such stories rest ultimately on natural happenings that have been understood by primitive expectation to be manifestations of the divine. The story of the burning bush is, on such a view, an Israelite version of a burning bush story, which is used in the tradition in order to express the divine presence. The story arises from the pre-scientific outlook of the ancient Israelites who 'expected supernatural appearances and . . . were accustomed to explain many events and occurrences as manifestations of the divine' (J. P. Hyatt, *Exodus: New Century Bible*, Oliphants, page 72).

A quite different approach looks for the origin of the burning bush not in an actual observation by someone, but in terms of the growth of the tradition, and literary devices. The Hebrew word for bush (*sneh*) is reminiscent of the name Sinai (Hebrew *sinai*). It is thus possible that the author wished to prepare the reader for the later great revelation at Sinai (Exodus 19). He did not mention Sinai *by name* in chapter 3 (Horeb in verse 1 is regarded by some editors as a later gloss), but *alluded to it* in the word for bush. The flame is also an allusion to the fire in which God descended on to Sinai in 19:18. The connexion between 'bush' and 'Sinai' may have arisen in the oral tradition, but in the present narrative, the burning bush is a deliberate literary allusion to chapter 19. A variation on the same sort of approach would be simply to regard the bush as originating from the pun in Hebrew on 'bush' and 'Sinai'. The *burning* of the bush would originate from the association of angels of God with fire. Thus the Seraphim of Isaiah 6 may be fiery beings (Hebrew *sāraph* = to burn); the cherubim who guarded the tree of life had flaming swords (Genesis 3:24); the angel of God in Judges 6:21 caused an offering to be devoured by fire. It is clear from Exodus 3:2 that the fire is caused by an angel.

These differing explanations are once more only possible because objectives principles for discovering 'what really happened' are lacking. This makes it difficult to give sound guidance. I am inclined to rule out the approach that says that Moses himself saw something, because the narrative is based on third-hand and not a first-person tradition (see Introduction, page 15). The whole story is a kind of shorthand, and the exact 'mechanics' of Moses's call cannot be known. We can only state that our passage is typical of other accounts of the *presence* of God, and, like them, asserts the Israelite conviction that the mystery of the divine presence could be truly known in the world of human experience.

We must turn, then, from the question of 'what happened' to the question 'what does the story mean to convey?' Whatever the exact historical nature of the encounter which is here recorded, as portrayed in the Old Testament it takes place in the course of a man's ordinary routine life. A familiar object is suddenly seen in a new way; there is an awareness of the beauty and awesomeness of holiness, and a human life is entrusted with immense tasks which will bring heartache and failure. Similar themes can be found elsewhere in the Old Testament. Amos tells us (though he does not tell us how) that 'the Lord took me from following the flock, and the Lord said to me, "Go, prophesy to my people Israel"' (Amos 7:15). Isaiah whilst worshipping in the temple, was made aware of the awesomeness of God and was entrusted with a divine task (Isaiah 6). Presumably, worship for Isaiah, and herding the flock for Amos, were routine things, one day to be shot through with new significance. Similarly, our Exodus narrative at least seeks to express that wider experience of ancient Israel of a God who somehow breaks through into the ordinary things of this world, with the purpose of offering deliverance and judgement, through the commitment of those who will follow his call.

7

THE PLAGUES IN EGYPT

Exodus 7:14–10:29, 12:29–36

Here, for the first time, we meet a narrative that is concerned with the *power* of God. In the standard commentaries the plagues receive full treatment, and only general comments are needed here. Readers will find the commentaries by S. R. Driver (Cambridge Bible) and J. P.

Hyatt (New Century Bible) particularly helpful in their general approach to the plagues.

Although there are ten plagues, it has long been recognized that the present narrative is a combination of probably two originally independent sources, which largely, but not completely, overlapped. Thus the plague of boils stands only in the Priestly source, while the plague of flies and cattle-plague are found only in the Yahwistic source. Neither of these originally separate sources probably contained more than eight plagues. The plagues are also referred to in Psalm 78:44–51 and Psalm 105:28–36, where again there are slight differences in the order and nature of the plagues, and where not more than eight plagues are enumerated in either Psalm.

Our present narrative has a certain climactic structure. The requests of Moses to Pharaoh become more demanding, beginning with a request that the Israelites should make a three-day journey into the wilderness to offer sacrifice to God (5:3), and ending in the demand that the whole people, taking their possessions with them, should be allowed to go and serve God in the wilderness (10:24–26). The present narrative, then, has a literary and dramatic structure, although its various sources can be reasonably well discerned.

Interest has understandably centred on the plagues, and their explanation. Conservative commentators, many of whom deny that different sources underlie the narrative, often accept that the plagues were natural occurrences, and see the miracle as resting in the timing of the plagues. A series of natural disasters in Egypt coinciding with the escape of the Israelite slaves is seen as the hand of God in the Exodus process. That the basis in fact of the traditions of the plagues was a natural disaster or disasters is also recognized by most commentators who are not conservative in approach, but they would allow a long and complex process in the growth of the tradition to its present form.

In an appendix to his commentary, Hyatt sets out two attempts to account for the plagues in natural terms. One assumes that they occurred in a year when the level of the Nile was unusually low, and the other assumes the opposite, that the Nile was unusually high. Both explanations try to account for all the plagues recorded in Egypt happening in a comparatively short space of time. Hyatt is right, in my view, to be cautious about such explanations, which make no allowance for the variation in the number and nature of the plagues in the underlying sources or the Psalms traditions. On the basis of this latter evidence, indeed, it must be asserted that although there were undoubtedly some natural disasters in Egypt when a group of Israelite slaves escaped, the exact number and nature of the disasters can never be known. In the course of time, the number of natural disasters has probably been added to as the stories have been told and re-told.

In the complex process that lies between the original events and the narrative in Exodus, folk-tale elements have had their influence, and have left their mark. In folk-tales, a common way in which magic works is by transforming one substance into something else (in Cinderella a pumpkin becomes a coach). Transformations occur in the plagues stories. Thus, the river is transformed into blood, dust is transformed into lice and ashes are transformed into boils. The fact that in folk-tales the forces of magic work on the side of the hero or heroes helps us to understand how the stories of the plagues were influenced and shaped by the folk-tale tradition of the ancient Hebrews. Stories about the natural disasters at the time of the Exodus, advantageous to the Hebrews, matched easily with traditional folk-stories about magic forces assisting the hero. In the course of oral transmission, the plague stories received some of their folk-tale features, for example, the idea that some plagues were produced by a magic rod, and that others were transformations of one substance into another. They also probably received some of the dialogue that now accompanies them, and something of the dramatic form whereby as soon as one plague had ceased, without any effect on Pharaoh's attitude, the next plague was brought about.

To put the implications of the preceding paragraph bluntly, what is being said is that though the traditions of the plagues have a *basis* in fact, and their occurrence at the time of the Exodus can be regarded as miraculous, it is highly unlikely that the interviews between Pharaoh and Moses took place with the dialogue recorded in Exodus. It is highly unlikely that Moses or Aaron waved a rod, or their hand, in order to bring about the plagues. Although we can only guess at what really happened, the likelihood is that the Israelites made an escape from Egypt that was contrary to Egyptian desires at a time of upheaval and confusion accompanied by several natural disasters. We owe it to the development of the stories in the folk tradition that the highly confused situation at the time of the Exodus was interpreted and presented in terms of divine initiative in favour of the Hebrews, that the confusion of events was reduced to an ordered succession of plagues and interviews with Pharaoh, and that this dramatic structure was able to explore the character and obstinacy of Pharaoh.

So far, then, it has been suggested that the oral shaping of recollections about natural disasters at the time of the Exodus was responsible for the magical elements in the narratives in their final forms, and that such oral shaping made possible the theological dimensions which the stories now possess. We must also observe another, and different, process at work. It is generally acknowledged that in the Priestly version of the plagues, the miraculous or supernatural element is heightened in comparison with other sources. For example, this source sometimes adds that a particular plague was also achieved by the Egyptian magicians, although the latter were unable to stop the plague. In the first plague, the Priestly version (see the commentaries for this) describes how all water throughout Egypt turned into blood, whereas the Yahwistic source restricts the miracle to the waters of the Nile. The Priestly source, although containing early traditions, is agreed to have reached its final form latest of all sources, and its heightening of the miraculous is an example of the way in which the further one gets from happenings in point of time, the easier it is to heighten the supernatural. The Priestly account also no doubt wishes to emphasize the transcendence of God.

In conclusion, the moral question has to be raised whether we believe that God would have treated Pharaoh and the Egyptians in the way described in the narratives. In the case of the hardening of Pharaoh's heart, the narrative displays some subtlety, and in its final form there is an apparent contradiction between Pharaoh hardening his own heart (8:32) and God hardening Pharaoh's heart (9:12). The whole theme probably originated in the folklore stage when the dramatic need to present the plagues in a culminating series also required a reason, which was provided by Pharaoh's obstinacy. The final narrative, however, seeks to express both God's complete control over the destinies of men (that is, God hardened Pharaoh's heart), and the part that can be played by a man in shaping his own destiny and those of others (that is, Pharaoh hardened his own heart).

The other moral question is whether God would have smitten the Egyptians with plagues; or to put it another way, what did the Israelites think when they read that God had smitten their foes? I doubt whether we have here an example of Israel's debased moral and spiritual understanding compared with our own supposed higher modern insights. The sort of story in which the 'goody' finally defeats the 'baddy' has long been popular, and in any case is part of folk literature. In our modern society, this story is embodied in 'Westerns' and detective novels. When we, or our young children, thrill to see the 'baddies' being shot down by the 'goodies' on the television screen, we rejoice that good has triumphed, and do not reflect on the disgusting spectacle of murder and killing. The story has become for us a symbol of the triumph of good over evil, and we would not have the story end in any other way.

It is possible that the stories of the plagues had a similar function as they were told, and re-told, in ancient Israel. In times when Israel was in alliance with Egypt, or depended on her for help, the stories would not express God's hatred of Egyptians, but would rather symbolize the victory of God over whatever opposed his purposes. They came to express a belief in the victory of good over evil, on the part of a God whose nature it was to succour the needy and oppressed. But above all, the plagues were part of that wider happening which we call the Exodus, a pattern of events which had far-reaching implications for ancient Israel's consciousness as the people of God, and of her faith in God's power to fulfil his ancient promises. The stories therefore were not only symbolic of the victory of good over evil, but a constant reminder to Israel of God's call to serve him in the fight against evil.

8

THE PILLAR OF CLOUD AND FIRE

Exodus 13:21–22, 14:19, 24, 40:38
Numbers 9:15–23, 10:34, 14:14

The pillar of cloud by day and of fire by night is a symbol for the presence of God during the wilderness wanderings. In the Yahwistic source it is a symbol not of an active presence, but of how *God himself* led the Israelites through the wilderness when there was no other leader who knew the way. In the Priestly source, the divine presence seems less active (see especially Numbers 9:15–23). Here, the pillar of cloud covers the tabernacle by day, and the pillar of fire covers it by night when the Israelites are not journeying. The taking-up of the pillar from the tabernacle is a sign that the Israelites are to journey further (Numbers 9:22); its presence is a sign that the camp must remain where it is.

Only the most literalist view of the Bible can accept the narrative at its face value: that an unbroken pillar of cloud travelled at the head of the Israelite caravan, turning at night into a fire. Thus even conservative commentators have allowed themselves a certain freedom in the interpretation of the passage. For example, it has been suggested that a whirlwind sighted in or near the camp was used by God to assure the people of his presence. But even an interpretation that assumes that the pillar of cloud goes back to a whirlwind actually observed by the Israelites in the camp, has to allow that it is not the same as saying that a pillar of cloud actually guided the Israelites through the wilderness. Even on such a conservative view, then, the present narrative is more symbolically and theologically true than literally and historically accurate.

Many commentators have sought the origin of the pillar of cloud and fire in the custom of guiding caravans at night by a lighted brazier or lighted torches. However, it has been rightly objected to this suggestion that it does not explain the origin of the pillar of cloud by day. Neither does it account for the fact that where natural phenomena are the basis for belief in divine manifestations, these are natural phenomena that are unusual and awesome (such as volcanoes), and not in any case of human manufacture. Such a commonplace thing as a man-made torch or brazier is hardly likely to have given rise to a tradition such as that which is our concern here.

A rival theory to the torch or brazier theory is the volcano theory. One writer has cited the 1905 eruption of Vesuvius as a parallel. Apparently the eruption was preceded by the emission of a great cloud of smoke which was visible many miles away, and which seemed to become a pillar of fire at night as the red-hot interior of the volcano shone upwards. Such a phenomenon is more likely to give rise to something like our passage; but the objection to this theory can be raised that there was no volcanic activity in the area of the wilderness wanderings. However, the theory could still stand if it were assumed that volcanic activity, not necessarily anywhere near the wilderness of Sinai nor at the time of the wanderings, had provided a symbol for the divine presence in the folk literature of the ancient Hebrews and surrounding peoples, and that this symbol had been employed in the tradition to describe God's presence among his people in the wilderness. On this view, the important fact would be the Israelite conviction that God's presence had guided his people. The pillar of cloud and fire would be a *means* of expressing this fact. Yet another possibility that has been suggested is that the incense which ascended together with the smoke of offerings from sanctuaries, is the origin of the symbol.

It will be clear once more that a straightforward 'explaining away' of the supernatural will not do justice to the complexities of this tradition, and that ultimately, only a sympathetic theological approach will appreciate its real point. It expresses ancient Israel's conviction not merely of the presence of God, but of his active guiding and leadership through a difficult journey. It is no wonder that the wilderness has been likened to the earthly pilgrimage of religious people, a journey in which God's active presence and guidance have been experienced.

9

THE CROSSING OF THE RED SEA

Exodus 14:15–31

Two basic sources underlying this narrative can be discerned, the one emphasizing the supernatural more than the other. In the Priestly account, verses 15–19, 21a, 21d–23, 26, 28–29, the miracle of the parting of the sea is attributed directly to God. The Israelites walk on dry ground through the sea, which stands like a wall on either side of the path. The Yahwistic version attributes the parting of the sea to 'a strong east wind all the night' (verse 21b) after which the sea returned to its 'wonted flow' (verse 27 RV). However, the Yahwistic version does not lack a supernatural element. In verses 24–25, God causes havoc among the Egyptians; verse 25 may suggest simply that the chariot wheels of the Egyptians were clogged in the sand of the sea bed, but taken together with verse 24, verse 25 implies that in some direct, though unspecified way, God fought against the Egyptians. It is possible that verse 24 has been shaped by the common Old Testament theme that in Israel's battles against her foes, the part played by her armies was small while the part played by God was great (compare Judges 7).

It is to the Yahwistic account that interpreters have looked in their attempts to find a natural underlying cause of the miracle. The two explanations that have most readily suggested themselves have been tidal ebb and flow (on the basis of verse 27) and a hot dry wind (verse 21b), or a combination of both. Explanations in terms of volcanic activity have not commended themselves to more recent commentators. An insoluble aspect of the problem has been the lack of agreement among scholars (a lack of agreement occasioned by lack of firm evidence) as to the site of the deliverance; it is not possible to ascertain which natural explanations would be plausible in relation to the place of the happening.

But is it right to base an explanation in natural terms on the Yahwistic narrative? If, as in the escape from Egypt at the time of the plagues, the whole incident was one of chaos and confusion, who was there with time to observe the natural science aspects of the parting of the waters? Another possibility, then, is that the Yahwistic account is an attempted *Israelite natural explanation* of the miracle. Alternatively, if Exodus 15 is earlier than the Yahwistic account, this ancient poem may have given rise to the Yahwistic and Priestly versions of the crossing of the sea.

Exodus 15:8 reads

'At the blast of thy nostrils the waters piled up,
The floods stood up in a heap . . .'

It can be argued, but not of course proved, that the Yahwist took his east wind from the phrase 'the blast of thy nostrils' and that the Priestly writer based his account on the phrase 'the waters were piled up'. If this latter suggestion is true, it provides us with an example of a different sort of origin for a supernatural story, the case in which elements of an ancient poem are turned literally into a prose account of a miracle. A similar example would be that of the sun standing still during the battle near Gibeon (Joshua 10:12–13). Although it has been powerfully argued that the incident in Joshua rests on an eclipse, it seems more likely that an ancient poem in which Joshua called on the sun not to go down until he had achieved victory, was later made the basis of a prose account which took the poem literally.

Ultimately, it is impossible to achieve any certainty in a discussion of 'what really happened' at the crossing of the sea, though few scholars today doubt that somehow some Israelites escaped and some Egyptians perished at the sea.

Compared with our uncertainty of how exactly the deliverance happened, there is no doubt that the Israelites regarded the Red Sea escape as one of the greatest formative moments in their history. It convinced them that their God was the lord of nature, and they had a lively sense that his deliverance was an expression of his response to Israel's need, and nothing deserved on their part. This is why in both the Priestly and Yahwistic narratives, God's part in the deliverance is all-important, and Israel's part is negligible, if indeed Israel has any part to play.

In one sense, the *lasting influence* that the Red Sea deliverance has had in the life of Israel, ancient and modern is as remarkable as the deliverance itself. Although the deliverance does not differ in kind from many other Old Testament miracles (it is possible to explain it in terms of natural phenomena, so that the miraculous is the coincidence of the natural phenomena with Israel's attempt to escape) it is perhaps the miracle which is to be connected more closely than any other with the phenomenon of Israel as a people believing in its divine election and destiny. It resembles the resurrection in that it challenges us not only to think about the initial formative event, but also to account for the lasting influence of that event in the existence of a community which has so deeply affected the world at large.

10

THE BRAZEN SERPENT

Numbers 21:4–9

The episode of the brazen serpent is one in which the concern to discover the origin of the story has sometimes obscured the theological purpose of the narrative in its present form. As it stands, the story is a good sermon. The Israelites murmur against the deliverance from slavery which God has achieved for them, and in spite of his miraculous provision of water and bread (Exodus 16–17) argue that they lack these things and in any case have no taste for the manna. Their ungratefulness, and disregard for the things that God has provided, leads them into disaster. They are punished by a plague of deadly serpents, and quickly conclude that even the God whom they criticize must be approached if they are to get what they want—freedom from the threat of death through snake bite. Although it was not explicitly stated that the repentance of the people was insincere, this may be inferred from the fact that although God provided a way out for the people, the way out did not operate automatically and to the exclusion of any response on the part of an individual. In fact, the onus was on each person to look in trust at the symbol of God's healing which Moses erected.

The brazen serpent is mentioned in II Kings 18:4, where it is stated that during Hezekiah's reform, the king broke the object in pieces because people had burned incense to it. This passage connects the serpent with Moses. The most popular form of explanation of the incident in Numbers 21 has been that the story is an aetiology (explanatory story) justifying the worship of a serpent in, or in the neighbourhood of,

Jerusalem, by connecting it with Moses. Some have argued that the serpent cult was part of the pre-Israelite religion of Jerusalem, and that the Numbers 21 tradition was generated in order to legitimize the cult as part of Israel's faith. It must be emphasized that if this theory is correct, it tells us only about the *origin* of the story underlying Numbers 21:4–9, and does not account for the theological teaching of the narrative in its present form.

Other explanations have been more complex: perhaps the snakes were not actual snakes; the narrative varies between serpents (verse 7) and fiery serpents (verses 6, 8) and the latter may have been demonic beings which were to be warded off by the image which was set up in the camp. Another view is that the setting up of the image was an instance of imitative magic, designed to cure the Israelites from an actual plague of poisonous snakes. Others, again, have linked the story with the snake as a symbol of healing, as sometimes found in connexion with the god Asclepios.

It is more likely that the basis of the story lies in some incident in the wilderness, than in an aetiology legitimizing a pre-Israelite cult practice in Jerusalem. The trouble with labelling something an aetiology is that so many unanswerable questions are raised. Why was the object legitimized by being connected with Moses in particular? Why did the aetiology take the story form that it did? Better knowledge of how aetiologies work has led recent writers on the subject to argue that it is most usual for an *existing* story to be linked to an *existing* practice or fact, and to be seen as the explanation of the latter. It is rarer for a story in all its details to be 'generated' in order to explain what often only corresponds to *one* detail in the story. The association of the brazen serpent with Moses in II Kings 18:4 is likely to be correct historically, and this may be supported by the recent discoveries at Timnah. Here, copper workings have been discovered, as well as a Midianite tent shrine in which was a copper serpent. The connexion of Moses with Midian is well attested in the tradition (Exodus 18).

It goes without saying that as it stands, the story displays deep insight into the nature of human attitudes to God. It describes the ever-present drive in human nature which wishes to convert the things of God into personal advantage; it shows how quickly disregard for God can be replaced by requests for his help, either where all else has failed or where human contentment has been disrupted. In meeting such situations, the divine response is not to meet human need in exactly the way people want, but to meet it so that faith and trust in God are

47

renewed and strengthened. This, I believe, is the meaning of the story as it now stands, whatever the stages by which it reached its present form. In the Apocrypha, Wisdom 16:5 ff. takes up the passage, emphasizing that the purpose of the plague was to draw the people back to God, and that it was not the brazen serpent itself that healed, but God and his word (Wisdom 16:7, 12). In John 3:14, we may perhaps be entitled to interpret the allusion to Numbers 21:4–9 as follows: Nicodemus seems to have difficulty in believing that Jesus is a teacher sent from God. Although Jesus tries to help the enquirer to overcome his difficulties (John 3:8) he refers finally to our passage in order to emphasize that ultimately, there is no automatic divine deliverance, and that there is an onus on the individual to trust in God's promises.

11

GIDEON'S FLEECE

Judges 6:36–40

The story of Gideon contains a typical example of a tradition about the *presence* of God (Judges 6:11–24). All the features of similar traditions which already have been discussed (see page 14) are present. There is an apparent confusion between the angel of God and God himself; Gideon does not immediately recognize the angel as a supernatural being; the angel is associated with fire; Gideon finally realizes that he has seen an angel of God and expects to die. The comments on other similar passages, and in the Introduction, should help the reader here.

In contrast, the incident of Gideon's fleece is about the *power* of God. It is in no way deeply embedded in its context; it also interrupts the flow of the narrative from 6:35 to 7:1. It shows close affinities with popular folk-belief. The hero seeks a sign, and prays that a fleece left out overnight should be wet with dew, while the ground is dry. When this wish is granted, Gideon seeks further confirmation by asking for the fleece to remain dry, but for the ground to be wet. It goes against too much that is said elsewhere in the Old Testament about signs and trust in God that we should take the narrative at its face value. The story shows all the signs of being a piece of folklore which has entered into the Old Testament without being properly assimilated to the deeper theological insights often displayed by the editors. The request for a sign to be repeated with the conditions the opposite of what has just happened, can be paralleled from non-Israelite folk-belief and practice. Only in respect of the diffidence shown by Gideon in his dealings with God does the story contain anything of permanent value.

12

THE CALL OF SAMUEL

I Samuel 3:1–18

The story of the call of Samuel is a variation on traditions about the *presence* of God. In this case, there is no apparent confusion between God and his angel, perhaps because the incident is set inside the temple at Shiloh (verse 3). However, we do find the theme that the divine is not immediately recognized for what it is. Three times, Samuel mistakes the voice of God for that of Eli.

The question that some readers wish to ask is whether this was an audial experience on the part of Samuel, that is, whether he actually heard a voice calling and speaking to him. The narrative assumes that he did, and as I have said in the Introduction (page 15) we must allow that some people genuinely claim to have had such experiences. However, it is also possible that because this is an account based on the third-hand tradition of encounter between God and man, there has been a heightening of the directness of the communication in the story, and that if we had had a narrative stemming from a first-hand tradition of what Samuel experienced, the story would have taken a more indirect form.

There are also indications in the narrative that it has been shaped and rounded off by oral transmission or by deliberate literary device. The threefold repetition of an incident (verses 4–8) is typical of folk-tales, and serves to heighten the climax of the story, which is the message which Samuel receives from God. Samuel's response to God's calling:

'speak; for thy servant heareth'

has often been used as a prayer by those seeking God's will, and the fact that it was, in the narrative, a response taught by Eli to Samuel (verse 9) may suggest that it formed part of religious instruction from priests or parents to their children. Such instruction would reflect the Old Testament conviction, expressed powerfully in the whole incident, that God 'speaks' to his people, for consolation and for judgement.

13

THE PLAGUES BROUGHT UPON THE PHILISTINES BY THE ARK

I Samuel 5:1–7:1

It can be regarded as certain that at some stage during the late 11th century BC, the ark of the covenant was captured by the Philistines from the Israelites, and then later returned. The stories of I Samuel 5:1–7:1 give an explanation *why* the ark was returned. They tell of the *power* of the ark as a holy object, and thus indirectly of the power of God. Most commentators look for the origin of the traditions about why the ark was returned in popular stories about the ark and its power.

According to the tradition, the ark affected the Philistines in two or three ways. First, the image of the god Dagon fell down in his temple in Ashdod, and then was mutilated. Second, the people of Ashdod, and subsequently of other places to which the ark was sent, were smitten with some sort of ailment such as boils and haemorrhoids. Possibly, third, they were plagued with rats (cp. 5:6 RV margin and NEB text). In the account of the misfortunes of the statue of Dagon, the incident explains a custom observed by priests and worshippers at the temple of Dagon.

It is quite feasible that the reason why the Philistines returned the ark was that its capture coincided with an outbreak of plague possibly caused by rats. The golden symbols of the plagues (6:4, 18) which were returned with the ark would in this case be charm objects to ward off the afflictions. It is more difficult to comment on the misfortunes of Dagon's image. If the information of 5:5 that visitors to the temple avoided treading on the threshold is correct, and if this fact was known to the Israelites, the story of the mutilation of the idol could have arisen in order to explain the custom.

The whole narrative in its present form shows signs of theological editing. The plagues which afflicted the Philistines are likened to the plagues in Egypt (6:6), and a contrast is drawn between the Egyptians who did not respond to the power of God displayed in the plagues, and the Philistines who were prudent enough to return the ark. Although the aim of the narrative is to display the superior power of the God of Israel over other gods, the whole incident contains a warning for the people of God. The ark was lost in the first place because the Israelites believed that it guaranteed victory whatever their moral attitude might be

(I Samuel 4). In this, they were profoundly mistaken. The purpose of the stories of the Philistine misfortunes after their capture of the ark is to show that the God of Israel is still the victor in spite of his people's defeat. Indeed, the incident reinforces the point that the loss of the ark was God's will, and part of his plan to teach his people first, that their moral attitudes were important (compare I Samuel 2:12–3:21) and second, that God would sweep away any symbol of his presence that became a substitute for his presence, and that was manipulated for human gain. In this last sense, the whole incident looks forward to the loss of the Jerusalem temple in 587 BC and to the bitterness of exile in which Israel was forced, through suffering, to learn deeper lessons about the divine plan.

14

ELIJAH'S DROUGHT

I Kings 17–18

The traditions about Elijah and Elisha present some features not previously encountered. Although the stories are third-hand traditions, the directness of divine communication that usually characterizes such stories is absent. Whereas elsewhere we have 'The Lord said unto Moses' or 'The Lord said to Samuel', in the Elijah and Elisha cycles the matter is more indirect. The word of the Lord comes to Elijah (for example 17:2, 8), although we are not told how. The great revelation of God on Mount Horeb (I Kings 19) has a sense of transcendence and immanence, as well as mystery. Elisha on one occasion depends on a music-induced trance to receive a message from God (II Kings 3:15). Whatever may be the reason for this fundamental difference, Elijah and Elisha certainly mark a transition between the tradition about the great men of God of Israel's period before there was a king, and the tradition stemming from the prophets of the 8th century onwards. Elijah and Elisha were active at the time when historical records were being kept, and were involved in national and international politics. Whereas only the vaguest details about the life and character of Moses are known for certain, it is possible to build up a fuller picture of Elijah. At the same time, the figures of Elijah and Elisha have attracted to themselves the sort of miraculous tales that centre on the exploits of mysterious holy men. Thus, on the one hand, we are dealing, in Elijah, with a clear historical character, while on the other hand, aspects of his work have been undoubtedly embellished by folk tradition.

In discussing Elijah's drought, we are faced with this problem: if we accept the account as substantially true, then why not do the same for the nature miracles of Moses? This is a fair question. If we accept on the grounds of faith and philosophical theology that God is active in the world in response to the prayers of his servants, and that Elijah was one of a select group of people whose outsized demands and burning conviction had amazing results, then why not add Moses to that select group, and treat his demands for miracles in exactly the same way? In one sense, it cannot be denied that the plagues in Egypt can be treated in exactly the same way as Elijah's drought. Both sets of phenomena were meant to bring a hostile king to his senses. But if interpreters have not treated Moses and Elijah alike, the reason lies in the *nature* of the traditions about the two men. As has been pointed out (see page 40) the traditions about the plagues show signs of folk-tale influences both in form and content, and this leads me to regard them as *later reflections*, on historical happenings which cannot be clearly determined. The tradition of Elijah's drought, although some folk-tales have been *attached to it* (compare I Kings 17:8–24), shows no signs of influence by folk tradition, and it would have been hard for such a story to gain credence if a drought of severe proportions had not affected a large number of people, and been remembered for some time after.

It is difficult to say whether Elijah prayed that there should be no rain, or whether he interpreted a drought as being God's punishment. Possibly both suggestions have some truth. If we take the contest on Mount Carmel and the ending of the drought (I Kings 18:43–46) as part of the drought story, Elijah displays a combination of shrewd observation, and unwavering faith in God's response to the requests of his servants. It has often been pointed out that the best natural explanation of the fire from heaven is lightning, and that such lightning could precede the heavy rains that quickly followed the contest on Mount Carmel. I Kings 18:1 indicates a link between the reappearance of Elijah after his hiding away from Ahab, and the coming of rain. A good knowledge of climatic conditions could have been, on the human side, the signal for Elijah to return and to set up the contest on Mount Carmel. On the other hand, it would be in keeping with the character of Elijah that he make no great distinction between what experience had taught him, and what he felt God was leading him to do. The whole point of the contest on Mount Carmel was that it was to be an authentication of the power of the God of Israel, and this was only achieved in all honesty by a man of the deepest faith putting that faith at risk. There may have been thunder in the air, but the miracle was that the lightning struck where Elijah prayed that the fire of God would descend.

At the end of the drought story we have Elijah running perhaps some twenty miles, and reaching Jezreel before Ahab's chariot did. It is possible that Elijah achieved this remarkable feat. We have to remember that he was an ascetic man living a largely outdoor life, and he could well have possessed unusual physical powers. Such a fact would fit in well with his fiery devotion to God, as well as with the fact that folk-tales were later attracted to the traditions about him.

15

VARIOUS MIRACLES OF ELIJAH AND ELISHA

Elijah fed by ravens	(I Kings 17:3–7)
The barrel of meal and the cruse of oil	(I Kings 17:14–16)
Elijah restores a dead boy	(I Kings 17:17–24)
Elijah brings fire down from heaven on his would-be captors	(II Kings 1:9–16)
Elijah's mantle	(II Kings 2:8, 14)
Elisha purifies water	(II Kings 2:19–22)
Boys who revile Elisha are killed by bears	(II Kings 2:23–24)
The pot of oil	(II Kings 4:1–7)
Elisha restores the Shunammite's son	(II Kings 4:18–37)
Elisha's staff	(II Kings 4:29–31)
Elisha purifies poisoned food	(II Kings 4:38–41)
Elisha multiplies food	(II Kings 4:42–44)
Gehazi is struck with leprosy	(II Kings 5:20–27)
Elisha makes the axehead swim	(II Kings 6:1–7)
Elisha's bones restore a dead man	(II Kings 13:20–21)

It is convenient to take together some of the miracles recorded in the Elijah/Elisha cycles. An examination of their number and nature indicates that they constitute a unique block of material in the Old Testament. It is true that a number of miracles are recorded in the accounts of the wilderness wanderings, including the incidents of the manna, the quails and the provision of water from the rock; but these latter miracles can easily be explained in terms of the natural resources in the Sinai desert, and in any case, they have been so deeply assimilated into the distinctive theology of the Old Testament that their primary function is to teach lessons about obedience and faithfulness to God. What is unique about the Elijah/Elisha miracles is their quantity, and the fact that in many cases they have not been assimilated to the theological purposes of their wider context.

Some of the stories point clearly to folk-tale as their immediate source. The miracle of the pot of oil is a typical example of the way in which in folk-tales magic forces assist those in need. Although there is no doubt that Elijah sought refuge with a poor widow of Zarephath, the account of the miracle worked on her behalf to give her and her son food, is clearly a folk-tale. Elijah's destruction by fire of soldiers sent to capture him expresses the dislike in folk-tales of hostile royal officers, whilst the transference of Naaman's leprosy to Gehazi is a popular way of describing the punishment of a trickster. Because of the folklore origin of the stories, it is not surprising to find duplicate stories. Thus six of them have to do with the miraculous provision of food or the purifying of contaminated food and water. The six are the miracles of the ravens, the barrel of meal and cruse of oil, the pot of oil, the purifying of water, the purifying of poisoned food, and the multiplication of food. Both prophets restore a dead boy to life, and Elisha's bones resuscitate a dead man. Because of the partial overlap of the miracles attributed to Elijah and Elisha, some historians have argued that only one of them actually existed (there are other difficulties also about the reconstruction of the history of Israel in this period). However, the two figures are too firmly connected with trustworthy historical narratives in the biblical record to sustain such a view, and the reason why their miracles overlap somewhat is that both figures have attracted to themselves typical folk-tale motifs.

Although in many cases, it is now impossible to ascertain what, if anything, is the historical basis underlying the miracles, not all of the stories are to be regarded in the same way. The destruction of forty-two children by two she-bears (II Kings 2:23–24) has a circumstantial ring about it. In its present form, there may be some telescoping, in that the ravaging of children by she-bears may have been understood as a punishment for mocking the man of God sometime earlier; in the biblical version, the telescoping made the bears come out from a wood as soon as Elisha had uttered his curse. However, an historical basis can be credibly reconstructed here. In the stories of purifying water or food,

54

the historical basis may well be that men like Elijah and Elisha had the knowledge of what we today call herbalism. Such a holy man would be consulted by a city whose water supply was polluted.

Several of the incidents have been worked into larger contexts, so as to carry a theological message. The widow of Zarephath (I Kings 17) is a foreigner and not a believer in the God of Israel. Yet her readiness to help the man of God, even to her last food, contrasts with the attitude of persons like King Ahab and his steward Obadiah, the former of whom has rejected his God, and the latter of whom is reluctant to make any sacrifice for his faith (I Kings 18:7 ff.). One is incidentally reminded here of the sort of folk-tale in which a wish quoted by a stranger enables a humble person to be enriched, whereas calculating, well-to-do people are unable to turn the wish to their own advantage. The incident of Elijah bringing fire on his would-be captors was probably already well shaped in the folk tradition. One notes that the incident happened three times. In its present form, however, the incident teaches the inadvisability of insolence to the servants of God, and counsels humility (II Kings 1:3). The purpose of the account of Elijah's mantle is to show that Elisha has truly succeeded to Elijah's office, and that God has not left his people in Israel without a guardian, at a time when faith in the God of Israel is under severe attack.

We can say that taken together, these stories reflect something of the Old Testament belief that while much that happens in the world is reasonable and predictable, God, in his relation to the world causes the unexpected and the mysterious to happen, and thereby warns man against trying to exclude the creator from his creation.

16

THE ASCENSION OF ELIJAH

II Kings 2:1–18

The taking up to heaven of a hero beloved of the gods is a theme found in the ancient Near East outside Israel. Nor is the ascension of Elijah unique in the Old Testament, although it is certainly the only explicit account of such a happening. In Genesis 5:24 it is reported that 'Enoch walked with God: and he was not; for God took him', and some commentators have seen allusions to the 'taking' of a man by God to himself in Psalm 49:15—'But God will ransom my soul from the power of

Sheol: for he will receive me', and in Psalm 73:24—'Thou shalt guide me with thy counsel, And afterward thou wilt receive me to glory'. Possibly too in Psalm 16:10–11—'For thou dost not give me up to Sheol, or let thy godly one see the Pit. Thou dost show me the path of life, in thy presence there is fullness of joy, in thy right hand are pleasures for evermore'.

As it stands, the narrative of Elijah's ascension is compounded of a number of elements. First, it has often been noted that the main character in the story is not Elijah but Elisha, and that the episode amounts to a prophetic 'calling' of Elisha. In this connexion, the narrative makes a point about the need for loyalty and persistence: Elisha will only receive the blessing which he seeks if he stays close to Elijah until the end (verse 10), and he has to resist Elijah's attempts to leave him behind (verses 4, 6). A second theme, which was noticed under section 15 is that of Elijah's mantle and its magical properties; but here, it symbolizes the spirit of Elijah, and marks Elisha as the true successor of his master. Third, there is the phrase, 'My father, my father, the chariots of Israel and its horsemen!' (verse 12). This phrase is found also in II Kings 13:14 when it is said as Elisha's death is perceived to be near. There may also be an allusion to it in II Kings 6:17, where Elisha's servant sees that although he and his master are in danger, they are surrounded by heavenly hosts of horses and chariots. It has been suggested that the phrase expresses a conviction and a prayer: a conviction that so long as Elijah was among the people, the powers of God were available through him to protect the people who were faithful to God against the threats of Jezebel; and a prayer that this protection would not be withdrawn after Elijah's departure.

The general reader wishes to know 'what happened' and how the tradition of Elijah's ascension came into being. The likelihood is that the place and circumstances of Elijah's death were unknown. The tradition about him indicates that he led a roving life, and that while the groups of prophets at certain places (some of them are mentioned in this passage) regarded him as their master, he was often absent from them. It is possible that our passage contains a hint of a search to find his dead body (verse 16–18), although, in its present form, this incident expresses a contrast between the certainty of Elisha and the doubt of the other prophets about the fate of their master.

If the place and circumstances of Elijah's death were unknown, the story of his ascension would have grown up, first, with the help of the fact that the idea of being 'taken up' was not confined to Israel alone, and second, with the help of the phrase about the chariots and horsemen.

The theological importance of the narrative, however, is that it expresses a conviction that fellowship with God is something that cannot, in cases of men like Elijah, be severed by death. It is often said that the Israelites had no belief in Lie after death, and that all men were doomed to a shadowy existence in Sheol, where God's power and presence were questionable. But belief in the afterworld is often far from logical (many modern church-goers apparently see no logical contradiction in thinking both of a Last Judgement and of immediately entering God's nearer presence when they die), and while the overwhelming belief of ancient Israel was no doubt concerning the hopelessness of afterlife in Sheol, a small but separate strand, represented by the ascension of Elijah and possibly the other passages listed at the beginning of this section, implies otherwise.

Perhaps the point can be better put by saying that Israel's traditional belief was concerned most with the 'where' of the afterlife. Although there is an inescapable spatial element in the idea of being 'taken' to God, the main point is that it speaks of *quality* of relationship. Can fellowship with God such as that established by a man like Elijah be cut short by death? The answer of the Old Testament was 'no', although in giving this answer it did not work out any new geography of the hereafter. For Christians, indeed, the idea of fellowship with God which cannot be broken by death would perhaps be a better way of speaking than some of their traditional language about the afterlife. In the Old Testament, it is the quality of fellowship with God achieved by a rare soul like Elijah that endures. The New Testament goes further, and speaks of a relation with God which he *bestows* on human beings who are not great saints. According to the New Testament, death cannot separate us from the love of God which is in Christ Jesus (Romans 8:38–39).

17

THE HEALING OF NAAMAN

II Kings 5:1–19

Although the Hebrew word for 'leprosy' includes the disease which modern readers associate with this word, it also denoted in biblical times lesser skin disorders. (See the article 'Leprosy' in *Hastings Dictionary of the Bible*, 2nd edition in one volume, 1956). Naaman's complaint, which apparently did not bar him from all contact with other persons, was probably of the lesser type. However, the main point of the narrative is to stress the 'ordinariness' of the miracle, and the importance of obedience to those who speak in God's name. Naaman expects Elisha to act in a spectacular way in performing the miracle (verse 11); instead, he is asked to do a simple thing on his own, without his high rank being acknowledged by the prophet. Thus the miracle depends as much on Naaman's obedience and humility, as on Elijah's power. The whole narrative is interesting in comparison with other incidents in the Elijah/Elisha cycle, for it is a counter-balance to the more spectacular miracles. Just as the word which came to Elijah on Mount Carmel was not in the spectacular but in the unspectacular (I Kings 19:11-12), so here, quiet obedience to God's orders is indicated as the way of power.

The conclusion of the story, in which Naaman asks for some earth to take with him to symbolize the presence of God, is not necessarily a sign of primitiveness. Many modern people find it easier to pay respects to their departed loved ones by caring for a grave, than by seeing a name in a book of remembrance at a Crematorium, because the grave focuses their feelings in a way that a name in a book can not. So, similarly, it was asking a lot of a man like Naaman to worship the God of Israel without the help of a tangible symbol. But alongside these seemingly crude approaches to the divine presence, must be put passages such as I Kings 8:27:

> But will God indeed dwell on the earth? behold, heaven and the highest heaven cannot contain thee; how much less this house which I have built!

18

THE VISION OF WATERS
FLOWING FROM THE TEMPLE

Ezekiel 47:1-12

Several years ago, Professor Zimmerli of Göttingen completed a commentary on Ezekiel which had taken him 14 years to write, and which was finally 1,285 pages long; yet he has admitted that in spite of all his labours on the book, not to mention the labours of others, there remain many unsolved mysteries in connexion with it. Chapter 47:1–12 shares some of these problems. The Hebrew text has certain awkwardnesses and inconsistencies (see the standard commentaries), and the passage shares with many other parts of the prophecy the problem of how we are to understand the visions. Were they basically real visions experienced by a man of unusual psychical make-up, or are they simply literary devices; or are they a combination of both factors? Commentators are agreed on one point, however, that in spite of its technical difficulties, 47:1–12 contains a clear message.

In our explanations in this book, we have distinguished between narratives based on first- and third-hand tradition. 47:1–12 is probably based on first-hand tradition coming from the prophet himself, although we do not know how directly the prophet was involved in its actual composition and writing. Like other first-hand traditions we have considered, it has the quality of indirectness. The whole action is a vision, and God is represented by a heavenly interpreter.

The vision draws together many biblical symbols, as well as symbols from the geography of Palestine. The waters which trickled out from the Temple (verse 2) recall the words of Psalm 46:4, 'There is a river, whose streams make glad the city of God.'

In fact, no river as such flows anywhere near Jerusalem, and the words of Ezekiel 47:1–12 and Psalm 46 are probably an ancient Israelite expression of the widespread belief in the ancient Near East that from the place where God or the gods dwelt, there flowed a life-giving river or rivers. Genesis 2:10, which describes how a river flowed from the Garden of Eden, is another expression of the same idea. No doubt in ancient times the Jerusalem spring named Gihon was believed to be the visible sign in Jerusalem of the presence of the river of paradise beneath the city.

In opposition to the life-giving waters of the river of God, the passage mentions the deathly waters of the Salt or Dead Sea. These waters, more than 1,000 feet below sea level, and containing a mineral concentration of 24%—26%, support no life, and bring immediate death to any fish brought into them by the River Jordan, which discharges into the Dead Sea. Whatever may be the origin of the story of the destruction of Sodom and Gomorrah (Genesis 19), the story no doubt owes something of its content to the weird and inhospitable landscape which surrounds the Dead Sea, so that the latter may not only symbolize death, but also the depths of human wickedness for which the names Sodom and Gomorrah are Old Testament symbols.

The way in which Ezekiel 47:1–12 describes the healing and life-giving effects of the waters from the temple needs no further explanations and the main message is clear: God's power will turn death into life. Two points must be specially noted, however. The time at which the vision was written down was probably still a time of apparent defeat for Israel. The temple was probably in ruins, and the people of God in exile in Babylon. Yet the certainty of the prophet that God would be victorious was unshakable, and he expressed this conviction in one of the most powerful visions of the Old Testament.

Secondly, it has been noted that what issued from the temple was not the mighty river in which a man could swim, though that is what the waters became (verse 5), but a trickle (verse 2). This puzzle is not explained in the passage; indeed the fact that the whole incident is a vision makes such explanation inappropriate, for we expect odd things to happen in visions. The fact, however, that the waters begin in a trickle is a point of great importance. Like the parables of the seed growing secretly and the mustard seed in the New Testament, our passage warns us that God's ways and beginnings in the world are often small and ordinary, and it needs a visionary to see their ultimate effects and victory.

19

THE BURNING FIERY FURNACE

Daniel 3

The book of Daniel is set, according to its own information, in 6th century Babylon, where the Jews are in exile. However, it has long been believed by commentators that this setting is a literary device, and that in fact the book was written to encourage Jews to remain loyal to their faith in the face of the persecutions of Antiochus IV round about 165 BC. The bulk of the material was probably from the outset symbolic or allegorical in character, and although some of the incidents in the stories may owe something to deeds that kings had done, or sufferings which Jews had suffered, there is no need for us to ask the question 'what really happened?' That question is no more appropriate here than in respect of Ezekiel 47:1–12 (see section 18).

The story of Shadrach, Meshach and Abed-nego is probably an example of the martyr type of story. Because Daniel plays no part in it, it may once have existed independently of the other material in the book, in some form or other. The story contains two main messages: first, that in God's world, however the forces opposed to God may seem to triumph and to defeat God's servants who remain loyal, the truth is that God and his servants are really victorious. The second message is that God's enemies are often reconciled to him through the sufferings of his servants.

In the incident of the burning fiery furnace, the miraculous elements are deliberately heightened so as to express the conviction that God alone is ultimately victorious. The heat of the furnace kills the men whose task it is to throw the prisoners into it (verse 22), and the king sees a fourth man, a divine messenger who symbolizes the presence and power of God, walking with the other three, all of whom are unharmed. Thus Shadrach, Meshach and Abed-nego have a happy outcome to their ordeal. Yet the account is not foolhardy enough to promise that this will be the case for every one of God's servants in similar positions. The three heroes assert (verses 17–18):

> our God whom we serve is able to deliver us from the burning fiery furnace ... But if not, be it known to you, O King, that we will not serve your gods ...

The words 'but if not' recognize that for many, even possibly for all of God's servants, there will be no miraculous deliverance. But taken with the story that follows, the words 'but if not' imply that the God who delivered Shadrach, Meshach and Abed-nego *from* death, will not allow other servants of his to be harmed *by* death.

The same points can be made about the second main message of the passage. In the story (though not in history) Shadrach, Meshach and Abed-nego lived to see Nebuchadnezzar acknowledge the God of Israel as the true God. Many servants of God would not have a similar satisfaction with regard to their persecutors. But the story invites them to trust that their sufferings will not be wasted.

The sceptic will ask whether all this is not really wishful thinking; nobody knows what happens after death, he will say, and incredible stories like that in Daniel 3 prove only that some people will believe any nonsense. However, the writers of Daniel 3 could look back over the history of Israel and see several examples of defeat turned into victory, and of persecutors reconciled to God. Jeremiah stands out as the supreme failure who was victorious (though he did not appreciate his victory), while in Isaiah 52:13 ff., those who have persecuted the Servant of God confess that they had been healed through his sufferings. Thus our story draws upon, and sums up, in a sort of parable, Israel's past experience of God at work. The exaggerations of the miraculous which the story contains serve to express the underlying conviction in the reality of unseen power. The story also looks forward to the New Testament in the way in which it brings together the role of suffering laid upon God's servants and the certainty of victory in what appears to the world to be defeat.

III ACTIVITY SUGGESTIONS

The aim of the following material is to enable readers, singly, or in groups, to test out some of the points explained in the Introduction and the examples. For instance, many people are bothered by the fact that if they decide that one miracle in the Old Testament is based on uncertain historical evidence, this seems to cast doubt on all the miracles. Section I attempts to give readers *objective* criteria for distinguishing, on literary grounds, between types of miracle story, as a preliminary to drawing conclusions about 'what happened'. The other sections deal with differences between narratives about the *power* of God and his *presence*, and with narratives based on first-hand and third-hand tradition.

Each section will need a good deal of time—at least two hours—if it is to be done properly. If the sections are tackled as group activities, it may be possible to apportion the work. For example, in section I, members of the group could divide up the accounts between them, and then having answered the questions separately, collate the results at the end. Others may prefer to discuss each question within the whole group.

I freely admit that I am open to the charge that I have selected the passages and framed the questions in such a way that the results will come out as I wish them! However, I believe the matter is not quite so subjective as that. My aim is that readers should be able to test out for themselves what this book is about, so that they can then apply the principles they learn to other parts of the Old Testament.

It is suggested that the activities are done either with the Revised Version or the Revised Standard Version of the Bible. Groups who used this material at the 'trial' stage, found that the verse numbering in the New English Bible sometimes differed from that in other versions, and that it was not always easy to see in the NEB where verses began and ended.

1

Task:
To examine the Elijah/Elisha miracles in order to see what types of stories are involved.

Material to be studied:

I Kings 17:1–24; 18:17–38, 41–46

II Kings 1:1–16; 2:1–18, 19–22, 23–25; 3:13–20; 4:1–7, 32–36,
    38–41, 42–44; 5:1–19; 6:1–7, 8–19; 13:20–21.

(It is appreciated that you have a lot of ground to cover, but the more
you cover, the fuller will be the results).

Method:
1. Make a list of the miracles that you find in these passages.
2. See which of the following descriptions apply to each miracle—
    (a) the story is brief and self-contained. (Put a+ if yes and a— if no,
         and similarly for the other assessments.)
    (b) the spectators are individuals or a small group of people.
    (c) the miracle is inexplicable in natural terms.
    (d) incidents are repeated three or several times.
    (e) the miracle demonstrates the power of the holy man rather than
         the direct power of God.
    (f) the miracle can be paralleled from folk-tales or legends known to
         you.
    (g) the incident expresses no distinctively biblical teaching about
         God.
    (h) put any other characteristic(s) that occur to you as you study the
         passages.

Now set out your results as follows:-

Name of miracle	a	b	c	d	e	f	g	h	
....	+	+			—	—			
....		—	—	+	+				etc.

Can you group the miracles on the basis of these results?

Would you care to make any comments or suggestions about historicity
on the basis of your results?

2

Task:
To study some of the passages about the *presence* of God, and to record
what you think are their common features.

Material to be studied:

Genesis 18:1–19:1; 28:10–17; 32:22–32;
Exodus 3:1–15; 33:17–23; 34:29–35;
I Kings 19:9–13a; Job 38:1–3 and 42:1–2, 5–6;
Ezekiel 1:4–28; Daniel 3:19–25.

Method:

1. Consider how the narratives treat the following points (note—each point will not necessarily apply to each narrative):
   (a) the feelings of the human person(s) involved.
   (b) the reactions of the human person(s) involved.
   (c) what natural phenomena or elements accompany the divine presence?
   (d) how are these natural phenomena or elements used in the story?
   (e) is the presence of God clearly described or
      (i) is God 'confused' with angels or messengers?
      (ii) are qualifying words, such as 'like', 'in the likeness of', 'as it were' used?
   (f) are there any other common features to be found in *at least three* or more of the stories?
2. Describe in your own words what you think is most striking about these passages, taken as a whole.

3

Task:

To examine some narratives based on first-hand tradition of experience of God, or communion with him, in the Old Testament.

Material to be studied:

Nehemiah 2:1–4	Jeremiah 1:11–19; 18:1–11
Psalm 22:1–11	Ezekiel 2:1–3:3
Psalm 51	Hosea 1:1–9
Isaiah 6:1–8	Amos 8:1–2

Method:

Consider the following questions in relation to the passages (not each question will necessarily apply in each case):
   (a) can the divine message be associated with some definite object or event in the person's life, if so, what?

(b) can you suggest a convincing psychological explanation for the human side of the encounter?

(c) detail the human emotions and reactions expressed in the passage.

(d) are any symbols or images used to express the divine presence; if so, what is their possible source?

(e) in what ways does your own experience match the experiences described here?

4

Task:
To examine some narratives based on third-hand tradition of experience of God, or communion with him, in the Old Testament.

Material to be studied:

Genesis 12:1–9	I Samuel 9:15–17
Genesis 26:24–25	I Samuel 14:36–46
Exodus 9:1–7	II Samuel 2:1–4
Exodus 25:1–9	II Kings 19:14–21
Leviticus 19:1–8	

Method:
Consider the following questions in relation to the passages (not each question will necessarily apply in each case):

(a) can the divine message be associated with some definite object or event in the life of the human person involved?

(b) is the encounter with God direct or indirect?

(c) does the passage describe the human emotions or reactions of the participant?

(d) are any symbols or images used to express the divine presence?

(e) does the passage give any indication about how the message might have come from God?

(f) compare your results with those under section 3. Can you make any generalizations, on the basis of the passages studied in both cases, of differences between the first-hand and third-hand accounts?

Part Two. NEW TESTAMENT
by Bruce Kaye

I INTRODUCTION

All four gospels tell a story of Jesus teaching a crowd in a lonely place and then feeding them in a miraculous way. Three of the gospels follow this story with another in which Jesus sends his disciples across to the other side of the sea of Galilee. They encounter a storm and are astounded to see Jesus walking towards them across the water. He enters the boat, the storm is stilled and soon afterwards they arrive at the other side of the sea. Both stories are difficult to believe as they stand. We don't walk on water, and we haven't seen anyone else do it. We have to prepare extra food if only a few unexpected people turn up for a meal; we certainly don't have the ability simply to manufacture an endless supply of food at will.

Response to such stories is of three kinds. Firstly unbelief, because it doesn't correspond to our own experience. Secondly, because we do not want to throw out a story in the Bible too quickly, we say that this was in ancient times when men did not understand nature as clearly as we do, and so they have simply left out any reference to the means by which these things were done, and have attributed them directly to Jesus whom they held in religious esteem. Thirdly, we suspect that the writers were biased because of the esteem in which they held Jesus, and that they invented stories of this kind in an attempt to improve his image. These three responses illustrate the preliminary questions we have to grapple with in any attempt to interpret the supernatural in the New Testament.

1. PRELIMINARY QUESTIONS

Almost inevitably we think that our experience of the world, or at least our understanding of the way the world works, is correct. Moreover we think that this is the way in which the world has always worked. Regularity is the norm. The farmer plants his seed in the expectation that something will grow. It is not simply because that is what happened last year, but rather because he has an understanding of nature which tells him that if he does one thing then certain other things will happen. This same understanding also tells him that if there is too much rain, or too little, then that too will have an effect on the crop. Therefore he seeks to control conditions so that he will obtain the best crop. He will farm in a scientific way.

Scientists, however, are not always certain to what extent they can be exactly sure about the way things work. The more they discover, the less certain some things seem to become. In the history of science it has been the nagging loose ends that have caused the trouble. Copernicus was not deliberately anti-establishment as a scientist; quite the contrary. It was simply that the way in which his contemporaries understood the relationship between the sun and the planets did not seem to him to give an entirely tidy explanation. There were some loose ends. The result was that he had to change the whole way in which observatory measurements were understood. The new way of seeing gave a better picture; it took account of more things. Loose ends and irregularities may suggest that the grid, the framework according to which we are viewing things, may be inadequate.

Our conviction about the regularity with which things repeat themselves in nature is dependent on this framework or grid. It is not that scientists have given up thinking in terms of regularity and order in nature, and are simply treating everything as if it were a totally random occurrence. Rather they are just a little less absolute, a little more cautious — not so much about nature as about our knowledge of the way it works.

This of itself is not a sufficient basis for admitting every odd story we come across. There may be many a slip between the event and the story about it. For example, are not at least some of the miracle stories in the New Testament accounted for by the unscientific attitudes of the people at that time? They did not understand about secondary causes, but simply believed that everything could be directly attributed to God. Since Jesus is regarded as divine, is it not reasonable to suppose that he should have things attributed to him in that direct way? Is it not true that miracle stories abound in this period, and this simply reflects an ancient scientific naïvety?

How far the ancients were naïve in this sense, and whether the New Testament miracle stories are really in the same category as other miracle stories of the time, is open to serious question. For the present we have to ask how God relates to the world. Is God known in the total history of man, and is there here a discernible regularity and continuity which speaks of the controlling hand of God? Or do we think that God is seen in the irregular and the discontinuous, and that in such circumstances he in some sense intervenes? If we think that God

70

is known only in the irregularities, then we may find ourselves at some point having to admit that there are not really many significant irregularities, and so God will have been squeezed out of the picture. If we say that God is known only in the regular and the continuous, then we are open to the charge that our belief in God does not really matter — it makes no difference in terms of what actually happens. On either count we seem to have lost God from the world of nature and events. Some indeed do think that this is the case, and that the real miracle, the real sign of the supernatural is the faith of the believer.

In many ways this idea that the real miracle is the faith of the believer has much to be said for it. It emphasizes the importance of the perception of the individual in seeing the hand of God at work. Christianity, however, has consistently thought of God as coming to men and revealing himself in the concrete and the historical. It is this commitment to the historical that causes so many difficulties in understanding for Christians. It would in some ways be much easier if they were not so committed to the historical, but to a philosophy or an ideal, because then they would not be so obviously open to the challenge of historical science. The New Testament also sees the whole creation as involved in God's saving purposes, and Paul speaks of the creation groaning in anticipation of its future redemption. So we cannot really abandon the natural world in our attempt to understand how God relates to the world. Three words sum up the way God acts in the world — sovereign, creative sustenance.

It is not the case that God simply keeps the world ticking along like some kind of clock, and that his creative activity is restricted to bringing the 'clock' into existence. Rather, God is creatively sustaining the world all the time. The regularity and continuity of the natural world is a measure of the regularity and continuity of God's character and way of doing things. Every event — no matter how regular it may seem — is a direct act of God. Some events seem more regular to us than others, and some of these irregular or startling events appear later to be a kind of creative bringing-together of other regularities that we can observe in the world. Thus the irregular is not at all excluded. The sovereignty of God in the world is of the same kind as that seen in the central acts of God in the life and death of Christ. That means that God does not exercise his sovereignty as some kind of coercive force, some kind of extreme end to the series of physical compulsions which we see in the internal relationships in the world around us. God's sovereignty is based on, and is exercised in terms of love. Thus the cross is the centre of the gospel message and the sign of God's love and man's judgement.

The commitment of Christianity to the historicity of its origins and continuing life, and to the presence of God in the world process, is clear in the New Testament, but its importance has varied from time to time in Christian thought. Thus the miracle stories of an odd and unnatural kind increased in early Christianity where the historical character of the 'origin events' of the Christian faith become less significant. It has sometimes been suggested that an increase in the miraculous stories about Jesus can be found within the development of the gospel tradition in the New Testament. This idea depends on what kind of chronological order is assumed for the gospels in the New Testament. This point has recently been widely discussed and is perhaps best left as an open question, but it is related to another matter which we have already touched on, namely how far the New Testament writers and their contemporaries were credulous in the matter of the scientific understanding of nature. The truth is that some ancient writers were more credulous than others. Parallels in non-Jewish literature contemporary with the New Testament miracle stories are not very helpful because they often refer to antiquity to explain some accepted tradition, rather than telling us about some recent or contemporary event. Furthermore, they are contained in sources which are often manifestly less discerning than the New Testament, and sometimes obviously fraudulent.

How far, then, are the New Testament stories reliable, historical accounts of what actually happened? If the early Christians came to believe that Jesus was the Christ, and if from their background they expected that the Christ would do miraculous things, then would they not be disposed to make up stories of Jesus doing miracles? This would be a fair assumption if we had good reason to think that the early Christians sat light to truthfulness in their attempts to relate the events of Jesus' life. Furthermore, these early Christians sought to proclaim and defend a faith which claimed to be rooted in historical events, and that the God and Father of our Lord Jesus Christ was himself the master of history and the world.

These preliminary considerations suggest that the basic problem with interpreting the supernatural in the New Testament is the same as with interpreting it today – how does God relate to the world? What does it mean to talk about God acting in the world and history? It is complicated in one important respect, namely, the fact that we have also to deal with the question of the reliability of the New Testament accounts.

There are therefore two questions we must consider. On the one hand there is the question at the New Testament end: what did the event mean to the New Testament writers? On the other hand there is the question at our end: what is the effect of our historical distance from the New Testament? Is their world any different from ours, and how do we understand the supernatural today? Before coming directly to these questions we need briefly to identify the different categories of material with which we have to deal.

2. CATEGORIES OF MATERIAL

Stories which refer to the supernatural are found throughout the New Testament, but they can be divided into different categories according to the different sorts of documents in which they are found. In the synoptic gospels there are seven categories:

1. Things that are simply out of the ordinary, e.g. the miraculous catch of fish (Luke 5:1–11).

2. Stories about angels, or voices which appear not to come from the normal sources, e.g. Joseph's dreams (Matthew 2:13–21).

3. Extraordinary insight or knowledge which has no apparent secondary source, e.g. Jesus' foretelling of his passion (Mark 8:31–33 etc).

4. Extraordinary, induced changes in natural things, e.g. the feeding of the multitude (Matthew 14:13–21 etc).

5. Healings which are exorcisms, e.g. the demoniac in the synagogue (Mark 1:23–27).

6. Healings which are physical, e.g. the blind man at Bethsaida (Mark 8:22–26).

7. References to supernatural things done by people other than Jesus or his disciples. The only account of such a thing is the story related by the disciples of a wandering exorcist (Mark 9:28–42).

In John's gospel these categories are present, except that there are no exorcisms, and John's vision of a dove at Jesus' baptism is the only miraculous thing not done by Jesus. There are only four healings, and two nature miracles (besides Jesus walking on the water and the large catch of fish after the resurrection). The material which can be regarded as simply discontinuous, or unusual, belongs chiefly to stories of incarnation and resurrection. Only one supernatural voice is heard, and that not by everyone present, and there is only one vision. There is, however, considerable material indicating remarkable insight without any apparent secondary cause. There are a number of summary statements about Jesus' works indicating how people, especially in Jerusalem, regard him. The outstanding characteristic of this gospel is the way in which a miracle story provides the central motif for extensive discourse material.

In the Acts of the Apostles the material falls into somewhat different categories.

1. Straightforward accounts of miraculous events. The effect of these is increased by their repetition in the narrative, and this is particularly the case with the re-telling on a number of occasions of the story of Jesus' resurrection and the inclusion (in summaries of the story's progress) of references to supernatural occurrences.

2. Stories of supernatural events which are directly linked with an explanation as to the significance of the miracle.

3. Supernatural interventions in the narrative, such as prophecies, visions or angels.

4. The three occurrences of the pentecostal outpouring of the Spirit.

5. A number of stories of supernatural events told in relation to magic.

In the rest of the New Testament the relevant material is much less, mainly because of the character of the documents. The interpretation of the apocalypse as a whole is really a different question.

Books on the miracles of the New Testament often pay attention to the terms used to refer to the miracles, and a few useful points can be made in this way. In the synoptic gospels the miracles of Jesus are called 'mighty works' *(dunameis)*, whereas in John they are more characteristically spoken of as 'signs' *(semeia)*. When the term 'sign' is used in the synoptic gospels in relation to miracles it is usually used in the singular, and usually with bad connotations, such as the scribes and Pharisees seeking a sign from Jesus.

John also refers to the miracles as 'works' *(erga)*. The term 'mighty work' or 'power' *(dunamis)* in the singular is used in relation to

74

miracles at Mark 5:30 to refer to the power which had gone out of Jesus in the healing of the woman with a haemorrage, and in Mark 9:39 in reference to the unknown exorcist whom the disciples wish to restrain. Such references in the singular do not occur in Matthew at all, but they do occur extensively in Luke-Acts. In Luke, and more so in Acts, the person performing the miracle acts very much as an independent agent who has power within himself to do the miracle. This is often in the context of magical healings, and reflects Luke's contact with Hellenistic magic. It is also worth noting that the term 'mighty works' in the synoptic gospels is used to describe Jesus' deeds as seen by the unbelieving or unseeing. In Acts the phrase 'mighty works, wonders and signs' is used in relation to Jesus' activity during his lifetime, and it also summarizes for Paul the signs of an apostle (2 Corinthians 12:12).

3. THE MEANING OF THE SUPERNATURAL FOR THE GOSPEL WRITERS

The New Testament writers display a sense of God present and active on virtually every page they have written, but their understanding of the more manifestly unusual aspects of the supernatural can be seen in those passages containing comment on the supernatural. There are different emphases in the various documents in the New Testament and we should identify these differences before asking how it affected their concept of God, and before we seek precisely to identify how they interpret the supernatural events which they describe.

For Matthew Jesus' mighty works are the sign of the fulfilment of the purposes of God in the history of Israel, and this fulfilment is centred in Jesus himself as the one who brings the kingdom of heaven. His exorcisms signal the presence of the kingdom, but the claims of Jesus are to be seen or accepted only by faith, and lack of faith is a bar to the performance of healing miracles. The rejection of Jesus by the Jews is a sign of disbelief in their own God. The whole range of Jesus' authority is given to the disciples in the mission of the twelve, and this mission anticipates the mission of the church, which must later testify to the presence of the kingdom of heaven.

In Luke we find a similar emphasis on the fulfilment of the scriptures which were read in the synagogue, but here it is focussed less on Jesus personally. There is more sense of Jesus' being the principal agent in the proclamation of the Kingdom of God. The mission, first of the twelve and then of the seventy, extends Jesus' ministry of proclaiming the Kingdom of God, and the unknown exorcist in Luke 9:49f. is not thought of as competing with Jesus, but rather as acting in line with Jesus' ministry. To reject Jesus' mission is to invite divine judgement. The theme of rejection of Jesus' mission is strongly emphasized by Luke, and it is rejection by men generally rather than the Jews specifically to which Luke draws attention. Sometimes the opposition to Jesus comes from Jews, as for example his rejection at Nazareth. In this case, however, Jesus provokes the opposition with somewhat aggresively stated reminders of God's blessing of Gentiles at the expense of Israelites in the Old Testament.

We meet also, in Luke, the idea that Jesus is able to perform miraculous healings because of a divine power which he has and which he can sense going out from him. This power is given to the disciples for their mission, and the use of this power is at their discretion. However, they are not to use such power in an improper way, and in any case the possession of such power is not as important as having their names in the book of life. This is an idea that is developed more fully in the Acts of the Apostles.

In Mark the miracles of Jesus have a significance in testifying who Jesus is, but this significance is only seen by those who have faith. Those who see the creator-redeemer God of the Old Testament present in Jesus are in sharp contrast to those who do not believe and to those who come seeking a sign from Jesus to test him. The Pharisees are the archetypes of such people. Mark has a very strong sense of Jesus as the incarnate Son of God, and thus the inability to do any healings is not because of the lack of faith on the part of those seeking to be healed, but rather to the refusal of the people to accept Jesus even though his teaching and miracles were acknowledged by them. Such refusal invites divine judgement. Mark sees Jesus' exorcisms as conflicts with and victories over Satan, and this is so because the conflict between God and Satan is brought to public notice as a conflict between Satan and God's incarnate Son. In this context there is less emphasis on the idea of fulfilment, particularly in relation to the Kingdom of God, which is such a noticeable feature of Matthew and Luke.

If we seek to go behind the question of what the events described meant to the evangelists, and ask how this affected their *concept of God*, we find a similar variety in combination with certain underlying agreements.

Matthew, with a strong sense of fulfilment, sees God as specially present and involved in the person of Jesus. Hence he sees Jesus as representing God to men, and thus calling for faith. This historical dimension to Matthew's understanding of God's presence in Jesus explains his interest in seeing this presence in the disciples, not only during Jesus' own lifetime but also afterwards in the mission of the church.

Luke shares Matthew's understanding that Jesus reveals God to men. However, Luke's emphasis is less exclusive than Matthew's. He sees the element of continuity with the Old Testament alongside the fulfilment in the present, and he sees God as present elsewhere. Jesus is not quite the exclusive presence of God that he is in Matthew. Because Luke sees God as truly and objectively present in the world, healings and miracles are not 'faith-healings', but the result of a real and objective power which can be given to Jesus' disciples, while residing also in Jesus himself. Similarly the Kingdom of God is not exclusively present in Jesus, but is present in the mission of the disciples. Luke understands God to be involved in a struggle with Satan, and this conflict is viewed more pessimistically by Luke when the scene of the struggle is this world. In this sense Luke thinks of the Kingdom of God as somewhat more otherworldly, or distant, than Matthew.

Mark shares with Matthew the sense that God is specially present in Jesus personally. He has, however, much less sense of fulfilment in this, and his orientation is much more the presence of the creator God. Like Luke he sees God and Satan in conflict, but when this conflict is being worked out in the events of Jesus' life, and particularly in his confrontations with the demons, Mark is much more optimistic, and sees God as decisively victorious in the here and now. Thus Jesus' mission brings judgement for those who reject it, and in some sense the Holy Spirit is an agent in the acceptance of Jesus.

The points we have noted about Luke's gospel are continued and developed in the Acts of the Apostles. Miracles are done by divine power. Sometimes Luke seems intent on denying that the apostles are workers of magic, yet at other times there appears to be a striking similarity between the miracles of the Christian missionaries and magical healings which are encountered. It seems clear that Luke has tried to come to terms with contemporary magic, and has done so differently in different contexts, though in all showing the superiority of the Christian mission and the word of the Kingdom which was being preached. This mission does meet with opposition, but such opposition is usually shown to be basely founded and no match for the power of the gospel. In this respect Acts is more optimistic in regard to the struggle between God and the forces of evil as it is being worked out in the here and now. God is at work in the mission, promoting and overseeing its progress.

When we focus on the understanding of God in Acts he seems to be somehow distant on the one hand, yet involved on the other. He seems distant in the sense that his representatives talk about him and do his work, and have his power at their disposal. Yet in this indirect way he is involved in the healings, the progress of the mission and judgement, particularly judgement within the Christian community.

Both Paul and John understand miraculous events as being of testimonial value for the message they proclaim, and they both see these signs as indications of God's being at work directly in what is happening. Both see the events of Jesus' life and death as the fulfilment of the Old Testament, though John makes more use of this than Paul. John actually structures his gospel so as to express the testimonial value of the signs. Miracles in John often provide the central motif for the discourse material in the context, and the long interpretative discourses in the second half of the gospel build on the position reached by the 'Book of Signs' in the first half of the gospel (i.e. John 1–12).

The New Testament writers have therefore quite clear ideas about the meaning of the supernatural, and the events surrounding the life, death and resurrection of Jesus have conspicuously affected their understanding of God in his relationship with themselves and with the world. But does not this very fact suggest that we cannot rely on these writers in our attempts to discover what actually happened? Are they not too biased? Three points must be borne in mind in our investigation of this question.

i. Bias: the fact that a writer appears to be biased, or to have a distinctive point of view in his writing, does not mean that his work is to be regarded as unreliable. Nor does it mean that a later historian cannot use his work in trying to discover what actually happened. It simply means that this writer's work is similar to all the other literary sources with which the historian works.

ii. Canon: the fact that this or that document at a particular point in time was included in a list of documents which the Christian church called a 'canon' does not mean that the document can be thereafter or thereby regarded as more (or less!) reliable for the purposes of the historian. The historian must treat the material as he finds it, just as he would any other source.

iii. Historical awareness: the New Testament writers appear to have an historical awareness as to both their distance from Jesus' lifetime and the character of their own writing. The loss of this historical awareness on the part of later Christian writers corresponds to an increase in stories about the supernatural, in relation both to Jesus and his associates, and to great Christian leaders of the day.

4. THE MEANING OF THE SUPERNATURAL TODAY

In many ways the identification of what happened, and what it meant to the New Testament writers, is a relatively simple matter compared with the task of saying what these supernatural things might mean today. Dealing with this requires us to deal firstly with the fact of the distance from us of the New Testament. While we may assume that the natural world works in much the same way today as it did then, our understanding of that world is very different. There is, however, a greater problem. It comes from the realization that our understanding of the supernatural is really only one aspect of the problem of understanding the natural, that is, the world.

For a long time Christians and others have thought of the world as a system which was more or less completely intelligible in terms of its own inner relationships. Thus secondary causes were all that were needed to explain natural phenomena, and the primary cause of 'God' was not at all necessary to explain the way the world worked. In this way 'God' becomes an optional extra, a matter of 'the way I see things', and not part of the fundamental or necessary understanding of the world. Thus nature and faith operate for many in quite different spheres.

Two considerations lead us to think that this is not adequate. On the one hand the understanding of the scientist is not mechanistic today in the way it used to be. The world appears to be much more open-ended, and our knowledge of it much less understood in terms of a kind of 'closed system'. On the other hand there is the theological consideration that Christianity is committed to the historical, and to the idea that God is actively and creatively sustaining the world. In other words, it is committed to an incarnational way of thinking. This means that the very concept of 'super-natural' is open to some question if it is thought to imply that God somehow exists apart from the world and makes 'sorties' into the world on occasions. This idea of the supernatural is very much under threat and criticism today, not because the division of reality into God (the supernatural) and the natural (or empirical) is under threat, but because in an empirical mentality the supernatural part of the picture is thought to be unnecessary. It is difficult to avoid the logic of this argument, given the framework within which it is conducted.

In our attempt to interpret the (so-called) supernatural in the New Testament we shall be concerned to identify how the New Testament writers themselves interpret these things, and to seek an understanding for today in terms of an open understanding of reality which is in line with modern scientific thinking, and with what I have called an incarnationalist way of thinking about the relation of God to the world.

The fundamental task is therefore the identification of the interpretative line in the New Testament, and the extension of that line to the present day. Before looking at the selection of passages in the second part of this book it may be worthwhile spelling out the general thrust of the interpretation that is given there in relation to particular incidents. The most important and pervasive direction in the New Testament writers' interpretation of the supernatural is away from marvels and wonders to morals and discipleship, but there is also a cluster of points around the focus on Jesus in the New Testament to which we should draw attention first of all.

The interpretative line of the New Testament writers, in regard to the supernatural events which they record, inevitably focuses on Jesus. There are six particular points which have significance for our understanding today and which we can list.

1. Jesus is historically distant because he lived in a particular place at a particular time. In this respect the Christian is always looking back to Jesus – there is a retrospective pole to his faith.

2. Related to this is the fact that the New Testament writers very specifically regard some events, and some supernatural events, as once-for-all events. They are events which centre on Jesus' historicity and the belief that in his historical incarnation he reveals, at that time and place, God to men.

3. As revealer of God, Jesus is also thought of as fulfilling the Old Testament, and therefore the revelation which he brings is understood in terms of that theological and moral tradition. It is worth remembering that the God of the Old Testament was pre-eminently a moral and ethical God. He called for obedience to his law before all else. The knowledge of God in the Old Testament is not theoretical or

speculative so much as practical and moral. This ethical monotheism distinguished Israel's faith from that of other nations, and the ethical thrust is carried forward fully by the New Testament writers.

4. When the supernatural is understood as pointing to Jesus, by the New Testament writers, they take that to mean that Jesus is Lord. Therefore Jesus is the touchstone for any experience of the truth. The experience of the Christian today is measured by its relation to the testimony of Jesus.

5. The word which Jesus gives is of abiding significance. His teaching is a vital part of the picture of him which the New Testament writers have.

6. The portrait of Jesus in the New Testament, in relation to which the writers interpret the supernatural, is of a public figure. His teaching is not secret, and his deeds are not hidden from public scrutiny. He is the subject of public knowledge, and subject to historical investigation. The origins of Christianity in Jesus were not things done in a corner, but openly and publicly. This means that in its origins Christianity is in opposition to superstition and secret knowledge, or secret experiences which cannot be shared and witnessed in the public arena.

When we say that the thrust of the interpretation of the supernatural is away from marvels to morals, we are simply drawing attention to the central character of Christianity generally. There are five particular points here which can be listed.

1. Marvels, as oddities in the normal course of events, are in no way excluded by the New Testament understanding. On the contrary they are accepted, and within a Christian understanding they are perfectly possible. However, they are accepted for what they are — oddities, irregularities, discontinuities in the way the world is normally experienced and understood. The odd or inexplicable is not defined with any great precision by Christianity. The 'beyond' in human experience is accepted by the Christian, while remaining agnostic as to its precise and detailed definition.

2. The New Testament writers, in dealing with the supernatural, point away from the marvel and the wonder, the odd and the irregular. The active and volitional thrust of these writers in regard to the supernatural is moral. They call for repentance, they point to the demand to

show love and compassion to all creatures. This is because the central commanding picture of Jesus, in terms of what he calls for from men, is ethical. The Christian is thus called to commitment to Jesus in the way in which he lives his life.

3. Part of this commitment is the task of preaching the gospel to all creatures. This is not really distinct from the preceding point, since the gospel of forgiveness and repentance which the Christian proclaims is part of the Christian's discipleship to Jesus. That discipleship involves love for others, and that implies love at the point of their need of forgiveness and repentance.

4. Religious experience, as with any other kind of human experience, is readily and openly accepted in the New Testament. However, that experience, like other experiences, must always be seen in relation to Jesus' witness to God and his call to discipleship. If what we call religious experience can be positively interpreted in relation to Jesus' call to discipleship, then the Christian accepts it in his life positively and directs its impulses towards the fulfilling of his Christian calling. If, however, such experiences cannot be thus positively interpreted and used, then the Christian is bound to set them aside as at best less than helpful, at worst as evil. The fact that an experience is called religious, for whatever reasons, does not make it one jot more useful in the Christian's discipleship.

5. Because the New Testament writers tend to adopt a straightforward view of human experience, and describe the experience of Jesus and others in straightforward terms, the modern Christian can often identify directly with the experience described. The common character of human experience in very different times and cultures makes such an identification possible. The temptation of Jesus to use faithless means to achieve the goal of his mission is a good example of this.

It ought not to surprise us that these points, in sum, direct our attention to Jesus himself and his call to discipleship. After all, if the New Testament writers have at the heart of their faith and life a commitment to Jesus and his way, then they are bound to interpret the whole of their experience in terms of that commitment. That they interpret the supernatural in their experience so consistently, and completely, in this fashion ought to remind the modern Christian that the heart of his Christianity is this same commitment to Jesus. No matter how attractive the diversions of so-called supernatural elements in his experience, he is called to a more fundamental and significant preoccupation. He is called to lay aside everything and follow Jesus the pioneer and perfector of his faith.

II SELECT PASSAGES

1

THE BIRTH OF JESUS

Matthew 1:18; Luke 2:1–7

The birth of Jesus is told only in Matthew and Luke. The fact that his mother was a virgin is never referred to in the New Testament outside these infancy stories—indeed his birth is scarcely referred to. The birth of a child to a virgin is unknown in Jewish traditions of the day, though we are familiar with stories of this kind from Greek traditions. The meaning of these stories of Jesus' birth to the New Testament writers is to be found within the stories themselves. It is significant that Matthew and Luke give their stories noticeably different emphases.

Matthew has the genealogy of Jesus first and then tells the story of Jesus' birth from the standpoint of Joseph. Jesus' birth is followed by the visit of the Magi and then the flight of Jesus with his parents to Egypt and their return later to Nazareth. In the story the focus is very much on Jesus individually. In his own person, and his experiences, he fulfils the destiny of Israel, and he fulfils what God had previously said through his prophets. This sense of fulfilment is heightened by the revelations that come to people in the story by way of dreams: Joseph as to whether he should marry Mary, the Magi as to whether they should return to Herod, Joseph that he should take the child and mother to Egypt and then later that he should return. Similarly the Magi are guided by a star, and the seers in Jerusalem come up with an unprecedented conclusion that the Messiah was to be born in Bethlehem.

On the particular question of the virgin birth as fulfilment we should note that the prophecy in Isaiah 7:14 does not refer to a virgin birth in the technical sense in which Matthew understands Jesus to have been born. In Isaiah 7 the prophet is simply referring to a normal birth, perhaps to one of the king's wives. The sign in Isaiah consists in the birth of the child after the events prophesied in Chapter 7 have

84

occurred, that is that Judah will not suffer at the hands of Ephraim and Syria who were at that time threatening Judah. As the child in Isaiah symbolized the provision of God for Judah, so now the baby Jesus symbolizes the provision of God for his people – 'he will save his people from their sins'.

In Luke the infancy stories of both Jesus and John the Baptist are woven into a much more elaborate tapestry, and the birth of Jesus is but one part of this. The genealogy is the prelude to Jesus' ministry in Luke and not to his birth and life as in Matthew. Luke sets his story in a wider historical context than does Matthew by relating his story to non-Jewish events. There is less focus on Jesus individually in comparison with Matthew, and Luke sees the birth of Jesus as the beginning of a group of decisive acts of God in history, in which Jesus plays but a part, albeit the central part. The story moves in the atmosphere of the people of the land such as Elizabeth, Anna, Simeon and the shepherds, rather than the Magi, Herod and the Temple seers.

Just as the story is told in somewhat different ways in each of these gospels so the interpretative imagery applied to the stories is somewhat different in each gospel. For Matthew the story is essentially linked with the 'Immanuel' prophecy from Isaiah 7, God is 'with us' in the person of Jesus. Jesus thus fulfils the destiny and hopes of Israel. For Luke Jesus' birth is part of a wider intervention by God into the affairs of men. The birth of Jesus and John signal the beginning of what God is doing on the stage of history, just as the ascension of Jesus at the end of Luke signals the end of this sort of action.

In both accounts the virgin birth draws attention to the unusual character of the birth, and thus of the child. There is nothing more than this in the stories themselves or anywhere in the New Testament. There is no suggestion that Jesus was born sinless by being born of a virgin, and from this point of view there was no necessity that he should have been born of a virgin. It was the view of some scholars at the beginning of this century that the earliest forms of the gospel tradition used by Luke contained no reference to the virgin birth, and that this was only introduced by adding Luke 1:34b to the text. Sometimes this suggestion has been combined with the view that the virgin birth was maintained in, or perhaps even introduced into the gospel tradition in order to express the divine and human natures of Jesus. This interpretation of the formation of the gospel tradition in the first century does not really commend itself for the simple reason that it presupposes ideas that hardly fit that time and place. Certainly

Church Fathers do later interpret the virgin birth in this way, however, and some argue for Jesus' sinless nature on this basis.

For Matthew, then, the virgin birth is simply a pointer to Jesus. For him it draws attention to this child, who on other grounds is regarded as the fulfiller of Israel's destiny and hopes, and is the means God uses to be present with his people. For Luke the virgin birth is a pointer to the events about to take place on the world stage. It is the beginning of the sentence of the incarnation of which the full stop is the ascension.

The birth of a child to a virgin cannot in principle be regarded as unique in the history of mankind, though if such a thing happened today we would regard it as something of a 'freak of nature' which, of course, is how we may quite properly regard Jesus' birth. However, the most important thing for the New Testament writers is not the 'freak of nature' but that to which they understood it to be pointing. Their focus is not on the birth as a wonder to attract attention to itself, but rather on what it was pointing to – the fulfilment of the destiny of Israel for Matthew and the coming universal gospel of Jesus for Luke.

Both these interpretations of the birth of Jesus automatically place Jesus' birth at an historical distance from us. Both interpretations point to a person and to events in a particular time and place, and not to some sort of abiding principle which might be transferred from one generation to the next. Nonetheless both interpretations have a significance today in that they provide a safeguard against tendencies in Christian faith which are not always helpful.

Matthew was concerned with the question of the relationship between Israel and the church. Jesus fulfils the destiny of Israel, and in turn inaugurates a group of his followers who will continue his ministry after his death. As they continue his ministry faithfully among the nations of the world then he is present with them with divine authority and power. Matthew's concern clearly belonged to the transition period when the church was still struggling to clarify its relationship with Judaism. That is not a question which presses upon Christians today. However, there is still the question of how Jesus is to be understood today. The understanding of God which is formulated in the Old Testament provides a framework within which Jesus can be placed. He is not a wandering miracle worker, nor a divine being with no antecedents. The importance of this for the understanding of Jesus today is that it means that he is to be understood within a particular moral tradition. The destiny of Israel is always bound up with the moral character of Jehovah and the character of the moral demands he makes upon his people. Similarly for Matthew the law is central to his understanding of Jesus, and the church in subsequent generations is re-called to the observance of the 'things that Jesus had commanded'.

Luke's concern with the universality of Christianity and the public character of the origin events of the gospel speaks to a slightly different continuing concern of the church. Most religions which emphasize personal faith run the risk of subjectivism and introspection. The church has often turned its back on the wider world and looked in upon itself. At such times the life of the church is often characterized by exclusiveness. Such introversion and private testing of experience and understanding are countered by the openness of the foundation events of Jesus' life and ministry. Luke's interpretation of Jesus' birth points to the public character of Christian origins. That interpretation today points to the public character of Christian experience and testimony, and to the fact that the Christian is directed into the world as the appropriate arena for his discipleship.

We note here a point that will recur in our study: that the interpretation of the supernatural in the New Testament by the New Testament writers moves away from the curious and spectacular to discipleship and the ethical.

2

THE TEMPTATION OF JESUS

Matthew 4: 1–11; Mark 1: 12–13; Luke 4: 1–13

The story of Jesus' temptation is found in all three synoptic gospels, and in roughly the same position in their account of Jesus. Mark does not give any details as to the character of the temptations, though he does say that he was tempted by Satan, the accuser of Jewish tradition. It is common to the synoptics that Jesus was driven into the wilderness by the Spirit, that he was there for the traditional period of forty days and that he was tempted by the devil.

Matthew and Luke in giving a more detailed account of the temptation reveal certain interpretative interests. First, the temptations are directed to the belief that Jesus is the Son of God. Second, they are orientated, in the answers given to the temptations, to the use of scripture in defending Jesus' messiahship. Third, the messiahship which is portrayed for Jesus here is that of a Son of God who trusts in God, who does not tempt but rather worships God. In other words a Son of God who is a model for the godly man. This is not particularly in line with their general picture of Christ as the Son of God, with the possible exception of Mark. This suggests that it is a piece of tradition about Jesus which has not been assimilated very much by the individual evangelists to their own particular interests or outlook. The point of the tradition is to emphasize the perfect model which Jesus has given to the Christian in his life of faith.

Given this particular thrust in this tradition about Jesus it is significant that the temptation narrative itself is cast in such a supernatural way. The devil is portrayed as a real person who comes to Jesus much as another person might come to him. Jesus and the devil are transported to the temple pinnacle, and to a high mountain to view the kingdoms of the world, in an entirely realistic manner. Yet the very terms of this last temptation (in Matthew) make it difficult to regard the narrative as a real description of what transpired in some sort of photographable way. The terms of the narrative are realistic and supernatural, but the very terms suggest to us that we should not take the narrative in such a simple fashion. This is the more important because the interpretative thrust of the narrative is away from such supernaturalism in the direction of a particular attitude to life; that is, an attitude which sees the whole of life as before God, trusting in his provision, obeying his commands and worshipping him alone.

The New Testament writers and those who created the tradition which they were using have already begun to interpret the story of Jesus' temptation. The very realism of the story as it has come down to us makes it difficult to take this realistic picture as the one which the tradition and the evangelists wished to convey as important. Already they are interpreting the story, and they are moving away from the thought of Jesus' being engaged, in any simple sense, in a struggle with a personal devil who is able to move around the creation like some first century Dr. Who.

Because of the actual details of the story which we have in the tradition, and of the interpretative work that has already been done in the formation of the tradition, the event with which we have to deal is the temptation experience of Jesus; that is to say, the fact that he was tempted to pursue his ministry in an unethical and self-asserting way. We have to deal here with an event that is all too familiar to us in religious and non-religious terms, the temptation to pursue an end in an improper way. For the Christian the temptation takes a more precise form – the temptation not to trust, obey and worship God. The temptation of Jesus comes just before his ministry commences. That ministry is the ministry of the Son of God, and it is a ministry in opposition to Satan. Here, however, we see that the Son of God effects his ministry by walking in faith and obedience to the commands of God. Jesus' life of obedience and humility is regularly held out to Christians as an example for them to follow, not only in the gospels, but in the writings of Paul and Peter as well. In the conflict with Satan, power and authority and victory are re-defined in terms of faith, obedience and humility. That this was a novel idea for the disciples is clear from such passages as Mark 10:35–45 where Peter and James seek a place in Jesus' kingdom as if it were a kingdom like any other. Jesus takes time and effort to tell his disciples that power and authority are to be found in service and humility. He calls people to take up their cross and follow him, thus indicating that discipleship is to walk in such humility and suffering as is symbolized by the cross.

It is apparent then that the temptation of Jesus is not to be extended along the direction of the simplistically supernaturalist elements in the story, but rather we are to follow the way in which those elements are actually used in the tradition, and the interpretative direction that is already set by the New Testament tradition. Once again we find the New Testament moving us away from wonder-working conceptions to the ethical and the practical.

3

THE DEMONIAC IN THE SYNAGOGUE

Mark 1:23–28; Luke 4:33–37

The story of the confrontation between Jesus and a demoniac in the synagogue at the beginning of his ministry is told by Mark and Luke but not by Matthew. In Mark the story is at the beginning of Jesus' Galilean ministry and is a typical first scene for that section of the gospel. In Luke the story comes at the start of Jesus' ministry in Palestine and is located, like Mark, in Capernaum. The two gospels have a great deal in common in the account of this initial impact of Jesus on Capernaum, but they deploy their material in slightly different interpretative directions.

In Mark the story of the demoniac in the synagogue is a generally typical incident and sets the scene for the reader for the following chapters of the gospel. In Luke, however, the story is part of the account of Jesus' acceptance in Capernaum, which is told in contrast to his rejection in Nazareth. The story tells of Jesus and his disciples going into the synagogue. Jesus taught the people with an authority that astonished those present. Then there was a man with an unclean spirit in the synagogue, who cried out against Jesus. Jesus rebuked the spirit which came out of the man. The spirit, in this exchange, had declared he knew Jesus as the Holy One of God, but Jesus had told him to be silent. The narrative is virtually identical in the two gospels, though the account of the response of the crowd is different and shows the interpretative line that is being taken by each evangelist. Mark has the crowd saying, 'What is this? A new teaching.' The teaching of Jesus and the power that he has over the demons are here welded together. What Mark is seeking to emphasize is that the secret about Jesus which will be finally revealed at the end of his gospel, and which he has included in the title of the gospel, is known to the demons because they know and are subject to the divine reality which is present amongst men in the person of Jesus.

Luke, however, is more concerned with the idea that the expulsion of the demon is a testimony to the word which Jesus has preached. The exorcism is a marvel to the bystanders and as such it speaks of the authority of Jesus and of the power of the preached word of Jesus.

In both gospels there is the clear assumption that Jesus is known to the demons, that he has authority over them, and that his divine authority is part of his being the Holy One of God. For Mark the story has a more precise significance. It is a window into the supernatural reality which Jesus comes to reveal. The story reflects the true nature of things. There are demons, they are real forces, and they belong to the same reality as the divinity of Jesus. The demons and Jesus' divinity are from the same realm. In this sense Mark represents a more static picture of things, in which Jesus embodies the presence and authority of God. Mark in this sense has a highly developed sense of the incarnation. For Luke the story is more in the nature of evidence of the power of Jesus, and therefore a commendation of his message. This is very much in line with the way in which Luke tends to interpret the miracles generally, and it is more dynamic a picture than that given by Mark.

The event to which the story refers has little reference to the sort of events to which we are accustomed. There are, from time to time, dramatic events which we read about in the newspapers which look very like the sort of thing contained in this story. That ought not to surprise us too much, since the fundamentals of human experience have not changed all that much, even though our way of understanding them has changed. However it is vital to notice how closely the evangelists have pieced together the story with their own interpretation of it. Luke is less committed to the literal interpretation of the details of the story in that he sees the demons as one only of a number of testimonies to Jesus and his message. If we were to find the testimony of the demons difficult to digest in the light of our contemporary understanding of reality, that does not matter too much since there are other evidences. With Mark, however, it is more difficult. For him, Jesus' divine character is tied in with the reality of the demons. The beyond of the incarnation is related to the beyond which the demons reveal.

The effect of our distance from the New Testament on our understanding of the story and its interpretation by Mark and Luke is not so significant with Luke as it is with Mark. Luke diminishes the problem because the evidence of the story is only one of a number of evidences. Furthermore there is a clear tradition in the gospels themselves which places less value on the testimony of such marvels. Jesus regularly discourages relying on signs, and will not perform them for his faithless contemporaries. However, with Mark the difficulty is increased, because the question of who Jesus is, and how we as Christians are to understand him continues to this day.

Our task is to see how the interpretative activity of the New Testament writers should guide us today. Where does their interpreting of the supernatural lead? Luke sees the testimony of the demons as part of the testimony of the whole creation to Jesus, whether that creation is understood and accepted as ordinary and everyday, or whether it is far from ordinary and is not really understood and taken as strangely outside or above the natural order of things. Even the history of nations and men concentrates upon the birth, life and death of Jesus, to testify to God. In this story of the demon, Luke sees it as part of a belief that the whole of creation—the known and the unknown— is under the lordship of Christ. The lordship consists of service and love.

The interpretative line to be found in the gospels generally, in the understanding of the lordship of Christ, is that of discipleship and service. Luke emphasizes within this the preaching of the word, the witnessing to Jesus in all parts of the earth. Luke thus leads us away from the marvellous and the spectacular to the humility and service of love. The disciple of Jesus the Lord is the one who shares in his trials, in the service of men and fellow creatures.

Mark, however, leads us on to slightly different lines in his interpreting activity. He raises for us the question of how to express the beyond, the unknown and incomprehensible in the world of our experience. Are we to make it into a substantial reality— to make a real demon out of it? Are we simply to let it rest in a mystery, and simply to remain agnostic about any close definition? The Christian of today is bound to take the second of these courses, not just because that is the current scientific attitude on the matter, but because he knows that the thought and activity of God is far greater than the greatest thoughts of the sons of men. He also knows that Christ draws him not to speculation so much as to discipleship.

If we ask more particularly, how we are to express the beyond of Jesus' person — our belief that he was not just a man — then we come to the heart of much contemporary theology. For the Christian who lives after the time of the historical Jesus, and after the resurrection, how is he to understand God's presence in Christ? Some have insisted that the divine in Christ was there independently and truly, but seem to find little place for any recognition of the subjective element in the faith which confesses Christ as Lord and God. Others have made the confession of Jesus as Lord so subjective that it hardly seems to be capable of open expression and shared understanding. It seems better to follow the line which the New Testament writers themselves set out in their interpreting of the supernatural aspects of Jesus' presence among men. Mark tells us that Jesus' immediate concern is the well-being of those whom he meets. He shows Jesus as full of compassion for the sick and the suffering, calling men to follow him. So rather than 'internalize' the divine in terms of subjective commitment, or 'externalize' it in terms of objective reality, I am suggesting that we should 'moralize' it. We should see the true expression of this 'beyond' in terms of a commitment to Jesus according to a certain life style, a certain morality, a commitment to the compassion of Christ in the person of our fellows.

A WIDOW'S SON AT NAIN

Luke 7:11–17

Just as the story of the healing of the blind man at Bethsaida is found only in Mark, so this story of the raising of the son of a widow at Nain is found only in Luke. Just as the story in Mark presented us with the need for a different interpretative approach from that used for stories which occur in more than one of the gospels, so we have to treat this story differently. Here we are concerned with the particularly Lucan interpretation of what is, on any reckoning, an outstanding story. There is hardly a story like it in the other gospels, and the only other raising of a dead person by Jesus which is recorded in the New Testament is the raising of Lazarus, in John's gospel.

In Luke the story comes just after the sermon on the plain (Luke 6:17–49) and the healing of the servant of a popular centurion in Capernaum. The story is followed by a section dealing with John the Baptist's question from prison as to whether Jesus is the one who is to come. This section is concerned to show that Jesus' ministry fulfils the hopes of the Jewish prophetic tradition, of which John was a part.

Luke has integrated this story into a theme which is of considerable importance to him, and which he wanted to bring out early in Jesus' ministry. The theme of fulfilment is not the dominant one which the story itself expresses, and Luke has taken the story as it came to him without a major re-drafting of the details to conform to his own interpretative interests. We can see the difference by looking first at the details of the story, and then at the way Luke has used and interpreted the story.

In the story Jesus comes to the city of Nain with his disciples and chances upon a funeral. The dead person is the son of a widow, and Jesus has compassion on her and tells her not to weep. He then restores the son to his mother, and the crowd respond by saying that a great prophet has arisen among them, and that God has visited his people. The words in the story, 'and he gave him to his mother' are similar to the words in 1 Kings 17:23 where Elijah restores a dead son to his mother, a widow at Zarephath. Even if there were not a verbal reminiscence of this Old Testament story the style and ethos of the story belong in the tradition of God visiting his people as protector of the fatherless and the widowed. The destitute and those without the normal means of support attract the compassion of Jehovah in the same way that the widow of Nain attracted Jesus' compassion. The conclusion of the crowd that a great prophet has arisen among them, and that God has visited them, is characteristic of the Elijah type of story in the Old Testament. It does not imply or indicate any sense that Jesus is the Messiah, or that this visitation is evidence for the arrival of the day of the Messiah. In other words, the idea of fulfilment does not arise in the details of the story.

Luke, however, has cast the story in a context which is entirely devoted to the use of the story as evidence for the coming of the day of the Messiah. The question of John the Baptist clearly has this intention; he is really asking if Jesus is the Messiah who will introduce the day of the Lord. In the answer which Jesus gives he refers to various things which were part of the prophetic expectation about the day of the Messiah. However he also includes a reference to the dead being raised. The Jewish expectation did not precisely have this point, though there was the expectation that all sickness and also death would be removed from God's people, just as had been the case in the wilderness. It is difficult to avoid the suggestion that Luke considered the story of the widow of Nain as the quite precise fulfilment of this expectation. The terms of Jesus' answer to John the Baptist are the same in Matthew, and were a firm and secure part of the early Christian tradition because of their significance in pointing to Jesus as the Messiah on the basis of his fulfilment of Jewish expectations.

Luke has somewhat stretched his geography in 7:17, in saying that the report of this event went throughout all Judea, and then introducing immediately the story of John's question from prison. Nain was in the far north in Galilee, and John was imprisoned in Machaerus in the south, on the western side of the Dead Sea. Luke is not always precise with his use of the names of the various geographical districts of Palestine. But the Judea reference in Luke 7:17 is almost certainly Luke's way of connecting the story of the widow's son in the north, with the question from John the Baptist in prison in the south. The real interest of Luke is the thought that Jesus is fulfilling the prophetic expectations, and this story of the raising of a dead man is very particular and pertinent evidence for this.

So we have a story which, in itself, does not have much indication of the theme of fulfilment, used by Luke to suit his own interpretative interests. Luke wishes to show that Jesus fulfils Old Testament prophetic expectations. He has a summary of these expectations derived from Jesus which includes an item which is not really part of the Jewish expectations. However, he also has to hand a story which supplies evidence for this Christian version of Jewish expectations and he uses that story in such a way that his interpretative interests are satisfied.

As an event in the normal course of things, we find the raising of a dead person to life quite incredible. The performance of such a thing with the use of highly complex and technical medical aids is not beyond belief, although it usually occurs in the case of one who has only recently died. The only difference in the case of the widow of Nain, and also the widow at Zarephath in the time of Elijah, is that the recorder of the event has seen it as an act of God. That is to say, they too have regarded it as incredible and have therefore come to think of it as something which can only be explained by reference to God. This implies an acceptance of the idea that God can act in nature in that way, and that nature is not such a closed system as to make it impossible.

In Luke the story has been given a much more particular meaning by the way in which Luke has interpreted it. He has not interpreted it as something which might be repeated by others. Rather he sees it as the very particular and unique testimony to the arrival of the day of the Messiah in the person of Jesus. In this sense Luke has made the story into a once-for-all event. It is only Jesus who does such things, because it is only in Jesus at this particular point in history that the day of the Messiah has come.

The effect of this interpretation by Luke is to root this event firmly in the past for us. It belongs only to the time of Jesus, and can only belong to that time. Furthermore its significance is not that it points to itself as a wonder to be marvelled at, but rather it points to Jesus as the Messiah, and the one to whom men are to be committed. It is very much in the Lucan style that this testimonial should come after the sermon on the plain. The testimony gives credence to Jesus as one to follow, and the word preached gives the content of that discipleship.

What this means today, if we are to follow Luke's interpretative direction, is that the Christian should be completely committed to the word of the Messiah and to compassion for those who are without support and defenseless. In modern societies where the welfare state and medical care take a considerable responsibility for the care of the deprived in society, the Christian might feel that in some sense he is not so obligated. On the contrary he is just as obligated, and he may seek to fulfil his obligation through the state instrumentalities. However, Luke's interpretative guidance to us is not simply to humanitarian works. Rather it is to commitment to Jesus of Nazareth as the Messiah, and to the expression of that commitment in the same kind of compassion as was shown by Jesus. Once again, the New Testament writer directs us away from the 'marvel' to the more important and the more fundamental. If the Christian today is to follow the interpreting of the supernatural that is followed in the New Testament then his commitment to Christ focuses on the ethical.

5

THE BLIND MAN AT BETHSAIDA

Mark 8:22–26

The story of the healing of a blind man at Bethsaida in Mark 8 is interesting to us in that it occurs only in Mark's gospel, so that we cannot make direct comparisons about the different ways in which the story is told in the different gospels (though we shall consider parallel material in Matthew). We therefore proceed by looking at the story in terms of its place within Mark and in relation to the thematic interests of Mark.

The story comes at the end of Jesus' ministry in Galilee, before the movement from Galilee to Jerusalem. In particular it finishes the section on Jesus and the Gentiles (Mark 7:24–8:26), but is immediately preceded by discussion with the disciples in which their slow understanding is highlighted. The story itself is distinctive in a number of ways. Jesus takes the blind man out of the village rather than healing him where, with him, he was confronted by the blind man's friends. Jesus also uses a peculiar method of healing. He spits on the man's eyes, and after a partial healing he lays his hands on them. The effect of this is to draw out the story and to show how the man was healed only in stages. It is a gradual healing in which the man himself participates and responds.

This drawn-out emphasis in the way Mark tells the story fits in with certain aspects of the context, and also with the paragraph which is parallel to this story in Matthew. Mark has just told us of the slowness of the disciples to perceive the significance of the feeding

miracles which Jesus had done: '... having eyes do you not see ... ?'
Mark then tells us of Jesus' enquiry of the disciples as to who men say
he is. On this occasion the culmination of the dialogue is Peter's confession that Jesus is the Christ. They do now perceive – having eyes
they do now see. In other words the healing of the blind man, placed
between these two paragraphs and at this point in Mark's gospel, has
the effect of being a demonstration of a deeper enlightenment that is
going on amongst the disciples.

It thus becomes interesting to note the parallel section in Matthew.
Matthew tells us of the discussion between Jesus and the disciples
about the leaven of the Pharisees and Sadducees, but Matthew draws
it out at the end of the discussion to emphasize that it is the teaching
of the Pharisees and Sadducees that Jesus has in mind, and to state
categorically that the disciples actually grasp what Jesus has said.
Matthew then goes on to the confession by Peter that Jesus is the
Christ. Matthew therefore has the dialogue on the slowness of the disciples to perceive set in the context of the unbelieving teaching of the
Pharisees and Sadducees. It ends with the disciples understanding and
is then immediately followed by the confession of faith. In Mark,
however, the disciples do not seem to perceive after the dialogue with
Jesus about the leaven of the Pharisees. The paragraph ends with
Jesus asking, 'Do you not yet believe?' The question is left in the air,
and before it is answered in terms of the confession of Peter at
Caesarea Philippi Mark has interposed the story of the gradual healing
of the blind man.

This story of the gradual healing of the blind man is thus, for Mark,
a demonstration of a more fundamental healing that is going on for the
disciples. The blind man and his healing provide for Mark narrative
demonstration of what is going on in the gospel story at this stage, and
which Matthew has given in the dialogue between Jesus and the disciples about the leaven of the Pharisees and Sadducees.

Whether or not Matthew has deliberately excluded this story is
difficult to say. It seems more likely that it was simply a tradition
which had probably been preserved by Christians in or near Bethsaida,
perhaps originally from the people who had brought the blind man to
Jesus. Mark has fastened on to this piece of 'floating tradition' and incorporated it into his development of the disciples' growing awareness
of who Jesus really was. In this way we can see that this story in Mark
is a very good example of the way in which a tradition about a
somewhat odd healing by Jesus is integrated into his concern to show

the disciples coming to faith in Jesus. Mark has given the story a meaning quite independent of the details of the story itself, and one which is wholly controlled by his own evangelistic intentions.

The way in which Jesus spits on the man's eyes and then lays his hands on him in the process of healing looks a little like the use of aids to healing. Modern medicine is fundamentally the attempt to cooperate in the healing process by the use of aids, but the aids in the story are of a very primitive kind and hardly come into the category of medical treatment. In any case these aspects of the story have not been included by Mark in order to make the healing more compatible with contemporary medical practice. They have been included for quite different reasons of thematic development. These aspects of the story do not therefore make it any easier to accommodate the event to our modern understanding of the way people are healed. That fundamental difference remains, and it is only resolved in terms of our understanding of how God relates to the natural order, and how God is present in Jesus.

Thus the thematic interest of Mark in the story is relevant to the concern of the modern Christian. Both are interested in the meaning of Jesus Christ to them. The modern Christian, like Mark himself, sees the whole event from the perspective of the resurrection. Mark has deliberately written about the disciples in such a way that they can be seen to be struggling with the question without that perspective. They are described in such a way that the path to faith in Jesus is not 'settled' by the resurrection. However, the dilemma of this situation is that even in the post-resurrection situation the disciples still have doubts and still show signs of having to learn the implications of commitment to Jesus. The same is true today. While, therefore, the perspective of the resurrection was not explicitly available to the disciples in the context of this story, it was in principle the perspective to which they were being drawn, and which they confessed as related in the following chapter.

Mark has used this story to show that the faith of the disciple of Christ is a growing and developing thing, and that the Christian disciple is always moving forward to new insights and new understandings of Christ. For the Christian today, committed in the same way, this is a corrective against triumphalism, and a call to press on in commitment and faith.

6

PETER'S PENNY

Matthew 17:22-27

This story about the miraculous provision of the coin needed to pay the Temple tax is found only in Matthew, whom we know has an interest in showing Jesus' fulfilment of the law and the prophets. The story comes after the transfiguration and at the end of a section (Matthew 13:53-17:27) on the rejection of the Christ despite the fact that there was good evidence, as Matthew has portrayed it, for accepting Jesus as the Christ. The story precedes Jesus' journey and challenge to Jerusalem. The story is thus set in the context of relations between Jesus and the Jews, and in this context has a fairly clear apologetic intention.

Within the story itself a number of interpretative images are used. Most important is the idea that the sons of the king are free. The imagery of the collection of taxation from all in the kingdom except those who were the sons of the king is drawn simply from Jesus' and Peter's understanding of the custom of the day. In raising this question Jesus displays remarkable insight into the conversation that Peter has just had with the tax collectors while he has been out. Jesus' instructions to Peter for the procurement of the necessary tax coin are given under the clear understanding that while Jesus and Peter are free, like sons of the king, from obligation to pay the tax, nonetheless this freedom is controlled by the principle of not giving offence. In the situation of the story this must mean that Jesus does not want to cause trouble for the tax collectors, in that the tax collectors would need to refer any refusal to pay to Jerusalem for decision. If the Jerusalem authorities ruled that Jesus and his disciples must pay then the tax collectors would be caught between Jesus and his opponents the Jewish authorities. Jesus is unwilling to allow this.

The legal discussion between Peter and Jesus which provides Matthew's interpretation of the provision of the tax coin is entirely in line with Matthew's interest in showing how Jesus is the fulfilment of Israel's destiny as the Son of God. On the other hand the provision of the tax coin by the astonishing method of fishing is quite out of line with the other miracles in the gospel tradition. Furthermore it is out of line with the moral discussion which is the real focus of the story in that it provides a way out by which the sons do not in fact pay the tax.

Yet the whole point of the freedom which Matthew espouses in the discussion is that that which is not a matter of obligation should nonetheless be done because of the overriding consideration of the position of the tax collectors. By the device of the fish effective payment is avoided.

The incident clearly means for Matthew that the sons are free, that Jesus' disciples are the sons of God and free from the constraints of Judaism. Such a point is of particular significance in a situation when there was still stress between Christians and Judaism in regard to the temple and its services and maintenance.

A quite rational and 'normal' explanation of the coin in the fish's mouth has been offered in the suggestion that if Peter took the first fish from the sea bed he would have a catfish. This would normally be thrown back by a pious Jew because it was unclean. Because it lived on the bottom of the lake it would be likely to have gathered up any glittering coin on the sea bed. However, this explanation simply changes the oddity from Jesus' capacity to produce a fish with a coin in its mouth to a fantastic series of coincidences. If the story is not regarded as involving such a series of coincidences, but that Jesus actually provided the fish, then the story inevitably attracts considerable doubt as to its veracity. Apart from its oddity in terms of our own experience, it is out of line with the way in which Jesus is elsewhere represented as performing miracles.

In any case the point of the story is quite clear from the interpretative dialogue which precedes. Indeed this is the central part of the story in that the acquisition of the coin is not actually related, and we read only of Jesus' instructions to Peter on the point. The interpretation by Matthew clearly refers to the tension between Jesus and the Jewish authorities, which is a dominant concern of this section of Matthew's gospel (and, indeed, a general concern of the whole gospel). The point of focus of this story, however, is the freedom of the sons of the king and the care to be taken by the sons in regard to those within Judaism who may be caught in the conflict between Judaism and the church. The church is here called on to act kindly towards Jews.

The point of the story is thus the moral point about the exercise of liberty according to love, in this case love for the tax collectors. This is a common problem in the New Testament and is expounded at considerable length in Romans 14 and 1 Corinthians 9–10. In 1 Corinthians care is to be taken for Christians from a pagan background, whereas in Matthew 17 it is Jews who are in mind. The principle, however, is the same: the Christian's behaviour is to be characterized by love and humility and not triumphant correctness. Once again we notice the way in which the New Testament interprets the supernatural away from 'wonder' and 'oddity' to the moral demands of Christian discipleship.

7

JESUS FORETELLS HIS PASSION

Matthew	16: 21–23	Mark	8: 31–33	Luke	9: 22
	17: 22–23		9: 30–32		9: 42–45
	20: 17–19		10: 33–34		18: 31–34

All three synoptic gospels record that on three separate occasions Jesus foretold that he would suffer in Jerusalem. There is general agreement amongst the gospels that the first two predictions come after the confession of Simon Peter at Caesarea Philippi and after the transfiguration. There is also general agreement that the third prediction comes just prior to the triumphal entry into Jerusalem, though in Luke this means that the second and third predictions are separated by the long journey narrative in a way that is not true of Matthew and Mark. There is also general agreement that the second and third predictions come in contexts which highlight the obtuseness of the disciples, to whom all three predictions are given.

Luke is the only evangelist to make use of these predictions in his passion narrative. The angels at the tomb of Jesus say to the women who had come to anoint Jesus, 'Remember how he told you, while he was still in Galilee, that the Son of Man must be delivered into the hands of sinful men, and be crucified, and on the third day rise' (24: 6–7, RSV). In the appearance story in Luke 24: 44–46 Jesus recalls for the disciples his teaching that the Christ should suffer and on the third day rise from the dead. This last reference mentions the Christ as the one who is to suffer and rise, rather than the Son of Man, but this may be due to the concern of Jesus in the context to show that this is all in fulfilment of the Old Testament. This passage also adds a reference to the universal mission which has not previously been part of the predictions of Jesus' passion, nor recollections of those predictions. This is probably due to Luke's view that the universal mission commences only when all the messianic expectations have been fulfilled in Jerusalem. There is also a brief reference found only at Luke 17:25 in which Jesus refers to his coming suffering as a necessary preliminary to the days of the Son of Man.

In order to see the pattern into which these predictions fall we can set them out as follows:

First Prediction. Matthew and Mark relate how Jesus begins to tell of his coming death and resurrection. Matthew refers this to Jesus himself, whereas Mark and Luke refer to the Son of Man.

Second Prediction. All three gospels refer to the Son of Man being delivered into the hands of men, Luke saying that the Son of Man is about to be delivered. All indicate that the prediction is given to the disciples, and register sorrow among them, but only Luke says that they are afraid to ask him about it.

Third Prediction. Matthew and Mark indicate that this prediction is given as they are on their way to Jerusalem. All three evangelists introduce for the first time in these predictions a reference to the Gentiles and scourging, but only Matthew and Mark mention any coming condemnation by scribes and elders. Luke emphasizes that the suffering that is to come is in fulfilment of what the prophets have written, and notes that the saying is hidden from the disciples.

The pattern of these predictions shows that Matthew and Mark tend to agree with each other as to the context of the predictions in detail, the details of Peter's rebuke, and the condemnation of Jesus at the hands of the scribes and elders. However, neither of these evangelists has what we might call a distinctive interpretative line which is manifested in these passages, whereas Luke does demonstrate a clear line. He, more than the others, sees the sufferings and resurrection of Jesus as fulfilment of the prophets. He sees these predictions as of much more significance than do the other evangelists, in the development of his understanding of the death and resurrection of Jesus as a necessary fulfilment, and he also sees the predictions as playing an important role in the disciples' growing awareness of this truth.

For the early church generally, then, there was widespread belief that Jesus said these things, and they come in the tradition as part of the disciples' developing awareness of Jesus' messiahship. Luke has a more particular interpretation of them. He sees them in terms of his understanding of Jesus' death and resurrection as a fulfilment of the Old Testament, and also (by means of his references to these predictions) of Jesus' own teaching. This is the more interesting in that Matthew is aware of such an idea, for he attributes to the Pharisees a knowledge of Jesus' teaching about his anticipated resurrection (Matthew 27:63), but Matthew himself makes no use of this teaching in his own interpretation of the passion.

If these predictions are simply testimony to Jesus' ability to see the way things were going and the likely consequences, then there is not much of a problem for us. This view has something to be said for it, in that the context in which the sayings are given draws attention to the obtuseness of the disciples in contrast to Jesus' perception. However, such a view could not really account for the references to the resurrection which might be taken as later reflections of the church.

The way in which Luke has interpreted and used these predictions makes them much more than testimony to Jesus' sagacity. Luke sees them as part of the proof that leads him to the conclusion that Jesus' death and resurrection were the fulfilment of divine intention. In this respect he places them alongside the prophetic use of the whole of the Old Testament and thus, in regarding them in the same category as the Old Testament, moves away from the possibility of Jesus' predictions being regarded as just a high level of human perception. It is clear that Luke regards Jesus as having a clear insight into God's plan for the Messiah, and that Jesus sees himself as this Messiah.

When we ask how Jesus might have come by such an understanding we are in some difficulty because while the idea of the Messiah suffering might be found in the Old Testament, the idea that he would rise from the dead is not at all clearly stated there. Later in the Acts of the Apostles the Christian preachers appeal to Psalms 16 and 110 in seeking to show that Jesus' resurrection was a fulfilment of the Old Testament.

Two things can be said about all this. First, the ability of Jesus to see into the future about his death and resurrection is seen by Luke as of the same order as the Old Testament prophets' ability to discern God's will or intentions as to the future. That capacity to identify the future is not unknown in other spheres of life, but it is very rare and mostly unreliable. Here the belief in Jesus' ability to do this is centrally fixed on the belief that he is the Messiah, and therefore it is regarded as of special and unique significance. The fact that this kind of prophecy largely disappears in orthodox Christianity is evidence for the belief that Jesus marks the fulfilment and the end of such prophecy. This is in line with the fact that Luke, who makes the most of this way of seeing Jesus' predictions, is also the one who has an ascension narrative which effectively draws a line between the mission of Jesus–his life, death and resurrection – on the one hand, and the continuing mission of Christians on the other.This is not to say that inspired utterances are no longer of significance in Christianity, but they are to be seen as just that – inspired utterances directed to the understanding and interpretation of the situation in which they occur and to which they are addressed.

Second, the interpretative line which is developed already in the New Testament about Jesus' role as a suffering Messiah moves in the direction of showing how Jesus is, in his suffering, the servant of his fellows. This is taken as an example for Christians to follow (e.g. Mark 10:35–45; or Philippians 2:5–11). In other words the prediction becomes part of a tradition of moral exhortation. It is once again the ethical which the New Testament interpretation of the supernatural is moving towards. That ethical feature is the more demanding, and the continuing point of application in subsequent generations.

8
THE FIG TREE CURSED AND WITHERED
Matthew 21:18–22; Mark 11:12–14, 20–26; (Luke 13:1–9)

The remarkable story of how Jesus cursed a fig tree which then withered and died is told by both Matthew and Mark, and a parable is told in Luke which refers to the cutting down of a fig tree that did not bear fruit. The details of the parable are so different from those of the story in Matthew and Mark, however, that there is probably no direct relationship between them in the development of the gospel tradition. Both parable and story do speak of judgement, and in the sense that they are concerned with that topic there is a relationship between them.

Both Matthew and Mark have the story upon Jesus' arrival in Jerusalem. In Matthew Jesus enters Jerusalem accompanied by the praise of the crowd, and then proceeds to cleanse the temple and declare that it should be a house of prayer. He heals some blind and lame people in the temple, and the chief priests and scribes complain about the children crying out 'Hosanna to the Son of David'. Jesus simply quotes Psalm 8 to the effect that God has brought perfect praise out of the mouths of babes and sucklings. He then retires to

Bethany. The next morning Jesus comes to the fig tree and when he finds no fruit on it he curses it and it withers at once. When the disciples ask about this they are told that if they have faith and pray then such things are possible. Jesus then continues on to the temple and is confronted by the chief priests and elders who want to know by what authority he does these things.

Mark, however, tells the story in a significantly different way. On the first day in Jerusalem Jesus simply comes into the temple and looks around, then retires to Bethany. On the second day he sees the fig tree in the morning and curses it. He then proceeds on to the temple where he hunts out the traders and money changers and teaches the people that the temple should be a house of prayer for all the nations. At this point the chief priests and scribes seek a way to destroy him. Jesus and his disciples retire to Bethany. On the way into the city the following morning the disciples notice that the fig tree has withered, and Peter recalls that it had been cursed by Jesus the day before. Jesus then gives much the same answer as is recorded in Luke, except that it is given a moral point by an insistence on forgiveness.

The order in which these events are given does not seem to indicate anything in particular for Matthew, though the withering of the fig tree is immediate and is thus in line with Matthew's interest in 'marvels'. In Mark, however, the story contains within it the account of the cleansing of the temple, and the hostility which this evokes is much greater in Mark than in Luke. The details of the story in each gospel also reflect the different 'interpretative interests of the evangelists. In Mark the cursing seems quite unrelated to Jesus' own personal needs; it is observed that it is not the season for figs. It may well be that the phrase 'for all the nations' given in Mark's account of Jesus' teaching about the temple as a place of prayer is related to the slightly different way in which the cursing of the fig tree is expressed. If the cursing of the fig tree and the cleansing of the temple are symbolically related in Mark's understanding, then the failure of Judaism and the temple in particular to provide a knowledge of God for the nations is the reason for God's judgement upon Israel. So the fig tree will no longer provide such fruit for anyone among the nations of the world.

The story of the cursing of the fig tree is thus interpreted in discernibly different ways by Matthew and Mark. The story itself shows the early Christian belief that the disciples of Christ could share the authority of Jesus by faith in prayer and by a godly life. Matthew, however, sees the story as more to do with Jesus personally and in terms of his being the forerunner of the wonder working disciple. Mark on the other hand has a much less personal and more programmatic view. The story indicates for him the judgement of Judaism.

In both Matthew and Mark the interpretative interests of the two evangelists have almost completely taken over the terms in which the story is told. Thus, while it is not actually said in so many words that Jesus withered the fig tree it is manifest that that is what they thought had happened. This is the only judgement-wonder in the gospels, though Luke tells us of the blinding of a magician by the name of Elymas who had opposed the mission of Paul and Barnabas in Paphos on Cyprus. This story in Acts 13 has many of the marks of Luke's contact with Hellenistic magic and of his attempt to come to terms with it. The story in the gospels of the fig tree is of an altogether different category, and is virtually unique in its destructive character. This opens the story to some doubt from a purely historical standpoint. It may be that a coincidence has been fastened on by the disciples in the first place and then the story of this has been taken up and developed by the evangelists in their own particular way. The dominant and clear message in the minds of the New Testament writers is thus the interpretative message which they seek to convey by means of this story.

Our distance from the New Testament puts this message into a different context and requires some re-stating. The judgement of God on the Judaism of the first century, or on the history of Israel up to the first century, is not as pressing an issue for us as it was for Jesus and the early disciples. For them it emphasized the momentous character of the change which Jesus' life, death and resurrection marked. No longer were they to have a religion which found its natural location and expression in the life and institutions of one nation, but rather a faith which broke down all national and social barriers and found its focus and life in the person of Jesus. The movement from national religion to universal faith was of the utmost significance for the first centuries of Christianity. Apart from the natural human temptations to revert to the previous situation the particular place of Judaism is not a pressing question for Christians today.

The attempt to locate God here or there is, however, a continuing human failing. Sometimes it is a particular church, a certain social expression of church life, a particular pattern of piety or even of social style and behaviour. Mark's interpretation of this supernatural story means for the Christian today that he is under constant challenge in two directions. On the one hand he is to express his discipleship in concrete terms – he must not only pray but he must forgive. On the other hand he must not think that one act of forgiveness or one expression of Christian faith at a particular point in time in particular circumstances can be taken as the unchanging pattern of Christian faith. Where there is no living faith the form is fit only for judgement. When there are no figs, the tree, even with its leaves, is only to be withered.

Interpreting the supernatural in the New Testament has once again led us to the ethical and the moral. But it is not a barren ethic to which we are led. It is an ethic which is an expression of, or a form of commitment to a living personal God. The Christian of today is led by the interpretative activity of the New Testament writers not to marvels, but to morals; such morals, however, as arise from living faith in Jesus. For the Christian that living faith is the really significant supernatural.

9

THE RESURRECTION OF JESUS

Matthew 28:1–20; Mark 16:1–8; Luke 24:1–52

The story of Jesus' resurrection is found in all the gospels, and belief in Jesus' resurrection is to be found throughout the whole of the New Testament. While there is a common general tradition that Jesus rose from the dead, there is considerable variety as to the details of the resurrection stories in the different gospels.

Matthew concludes his picture of the crucifixion with particular attention to the burial of Jesus and the setting of a guard on the tomb in order to prevent any activity on the part of Jesus' disciples which might be made the basis of a fraudulent claim that Jesus had risen from the dead. The resurrection narrative itself is told as an announcement of the fact of Jesus' resurrection by an angel. The story is very much in the form of a wonder story, the dramatic appearance of the angel, the earthquake, the rolling away of the stone as part of the signal of the presence of the angel. This leads on to the instruction for the disciples to go to Galilee where the great commission is given for the continuation of Jesus' ministry through the disciples. There is a parenthesis in Matthew 28:11–15 which deals with the guard and the charge of fraud that had been anticipated in the final part of the crucifixion narrative. This parenthesis reveals a clear apologetical theme in regard to the Jewish authorities.

In Mark the crucifixion detail of Jesus' burial by Joseph of Arimathea emphasizes that Jesus was in fact dead, and securely buried behind a large stone (Mark 15:46; 16:3). The resurrection narrative picks up these points by references to the fact that Jesus was crucified (Mark 16:6) and that having risen, he is not in the grave where he had been buried (Mark 16:6). Mark's resurrection narrative is much less of a wonder story than Matthew's, though like the latter it leads into the instruction for the disciples to go to Galilee.

Luke provides us with the longest resurrection narrative and the largest number of resurrection appearances. Matthew (aside from the great commission appearance) has only one brief appearance to the women who had visited the tomb, and that is only to confirm what they had been told at the tomb by the angel, and if with most scholars we regard Mark 16:8 as the end of his original account, then Mark has no resurrection appearances at all. The account of Jesus' death and burial in Luke has some of the details found in Matthew and Mark but they do not seem to have the same emphasis. Luke draws attention to the piety of the participants (compare his description of Joseph of Arimathea, in 23:50 f., with the briefer notice in Matthew 27:57 f. and Mark 15:43). As with Matthew and Mark there is no direct assertion of Jesus' resurrection, but a rhetorical question refers to Jesus' prophecy that he would rise from the dead (Luke 24:7 f.). The story of the women who first visit the tomb is dismissed by the rest of the disciples.

The first actual resurrection appearance of Jesus in Luke's account is to the two disciples on the road to Emmaus (Luke 24:13–32). As with the first section of Luke's account Jesus' resurrection is not asserted directly, but it is pointed to by recollection of the events, and then by the recalling of the teaching of the Old Testament about the necessity of suffering as the way to glory for the Messiah. The conclusion of the section, at which the disciples perceive that it is the risen Jesus who is with them, is arrived at again by recollection, this time of the characteristic way in which Jesus broke bread with them during his lifetime.

The conclusion to Luke's account of the resurrection is located in Jerusalem and is drawn out on the basis of the reported appearance of

Jesus to Simon, which is brought into relationship with the report of the two disciples who had been going to Emmaus (Luke 24:33–35). The *coup de grâce* in this developing picture is the appearance of Jesus to the group of disciples in Jerusalem just as they have reached the conclusion that Jesus has risen. Jesus appears in their midst and his identity is established (Luke 24:36–43), and then he teaches them from the Old Testament how the Messiah was expected to suffer, but unlike the comments to the two on the road to Emmaus this time Jesus also gives instruction about the universal mission and instructions to the disciples about their place in this mission. The gospel ends with an ascension account to show that the Messiah has come, and now gone, and his work is now to be continued by the disciples.

Luke's account of the resurrection is a very carefully constructed piece of writing, and by a series of episodes, each leading up to a conclusion, a final conclusion that Jesus has risen is reached in Luke 24:33 f. This conclusion is not just that Jesus has risen, but that he has risen in fulfilment of the Old Testament teaching about the role of the Messiah, and this is also in line with his own teaching given during his lifetime. The appeal to evidence which this structure displays is in line with Luke's general literary style. The location of the final resurrection *dénouement* and the ascension in Jerusalem are important to Luke's understanding of the Gentile mission. He sees the mission itself as proceeding from Jerusalem, from Israel, after the completion of the work of the Messiah, whereas for Matthew and Mark the role of Israel seems already to have passed with the end of the work of the Messiah, and they see the universal mission already detached from Israel and starting from Galilee of the Gentiles.

It has been impossible in this brief description of the various synoptic accounts of the resurrection to avoid drawing attention to the interpretative imagery that the various evangelists have used. We may note a number of other specific interpretative images which the evangelists have used. Matthew specifically mentions an earthquake in signalling the presence of the angel who has the message of Jesus' resurrection, and it is Matthew who tells us of the earthquake at the time of the crucifixion when the bodies of the saints were raised (Matthew 27:51 ff.). The apologetical intention in Matthew's account is directed against official Judaism. This purpose is pursued by showing that the reports of the soldiers that Jesus' resurrection is a fraud perpetrated by the disciples is false, and that it arises from a base motive of bribery. It is somewhat strange that there is little attempt made, as in Luke, to show that the resurrection was in fulfilment of the Old Testament, since that has been one of Matthew's main concerns throughout his gospel. Unlike Luke, who clearly indicates Jesus' departure from his disciples, Matthew has Jesus staying with his people to help them to continue his work.

Mark is brief and descriptive and evidential in character, whereas Luke's is a much more highly structured account. Two main themes dominate Luke's account of the resurrection: the resurrection fulfils both Old Testament messianic expectations and Jesus' own teaching, and the mission to the Gentiles begins only after the end of the life of the Messiah.

There appears to be no clear common understanding of the resurrection in terms of its indicating anything about Jesus as the Christ. The main common point in the synoptic accounts is the connexion between the resurrection and the mission, and this for the early church clearly indicates that the resurrection declares that Jesus' death is not the end. Jesus is significant for generations after the time of his incarnation. For Matthew the resurrection means that Judaism is gone, and Jesus is present with his people in the making of disciples. Like other events in his gospel Mark sees the resurrection as a kind of rhetorical question, somewhat dramatically put, the answer to which is that Jesus is the Son of God. For Luke the resurrection highlights the fulfilment of the Old Testament by Jesus and is the great and final act of the Messiah.

The picture of Jesus' resurrection in the synoptic gospels defies explanation in terms of our modern scientific understanding of the way in which physical bodies relate to one another. However, the texts themselves already know this since they relate quite inexplicable things about Jesus in his resurrection. They also show some reticence about detailed descriptions or explanations at this level. If we concede, with the texts, that Jesus' risen form was not strictly physical, then it is a much more open question as to how we might understand the stories in terms of our modern conceptions. That question is raised already in the texts, and we are bound to remain agnostic as to how Jesus existed after his resurrection.

The interpretative activity of the New Testament writers moves away from that question as not being of fundamental significance for them. They point to other things which are central for them. Mark comes nearest to the popular notion that the resurrection proved Jesus to be the Son of God. For Mark the resurrection raises in question form the identity of Jesus and, as elsewhere in his gospel, the implied answer is that Jesus is the Son of God. However, the resurrection for Mark is continuous with these other events in Jesus' life which raised that question, right from the first chapter when Jesus exorcized the man in the synagogue. The resurrection is thus not a great reversal of Jesus' death. This is especially clear in the fact that one important public confession that Jesus is the Son of God comes at the point of the crucifixion. Mark's point is that Jesus is the Son of God, that God is incarnate in Jesus. The point of Mark's resurrection narrative is that God is still present with men after Jesus' death, and for Christians living after the time of Jesus' life that is a vital point. God is still able to be present with men today, though his presence is a presence akin to that which the disciples knew in Jesus of Nazareth. As with the resurrection of Jesus, and the identification of Jesus as the Son of God during his lifetime by the disciples, the presence of God today is still a matter of faith. It is a matter that is stated by a question:- is this not God speaking to us? So for the modern Christian God's presence is always Jesus-like and discerned only by faith. In this sense the knowledge of God is always open to question and to doubt. Indeed, doubt is the other side of the coin of faith.

The particular line of interpretation developed by Matthew that Judaism is now gone, and that God is now present in the mission of Jesus' disciples, is not such a vital issue to the modern Christian. The break with Judaism is historically well behind him. But the implication of Matthew's point, that God's presence is now personal and not national, or more precisely institutional, is of significance to the modern Christian. The temptation to identify the institutions which have developed in Christian history with the presence of God is a continuing temptation. Whether it is the club of the Church of England, or the empire of the Roman Catholic Church, or the society of the denomination really makes no difference. To identify God's presence with man with any of these is to fall back into the error of the Judaism of Matthew's day.

Luke's interpretative line is of importance to the modern Christian because it points to the historical continuity between this generation and previous Christian experience. Luke emphasizes that the events of Jesus' life, and especially his resurrection, fulfil the Old Testament. This is not completely different from what God had been doing amongst men before. Indeed the thrust in Luke leads on to the

111

point central in Paul's thought that the Christian is someone who is caught up into the activity and purposes of God. The Christian today is assured by this view of the possibility of God's continuing activity in the world after Jesus' death. He is also assured of the continuity between his own experience of God now and the great salvation events of Jesus' life, death and resurrection.

The three synoptic gospels all relate the resurrection of Jesus to the universal mission in one way or another. If one were to identify one single common emphasis in the tradition this would be it. It means that Jesus' incarnation is not just for the first century, but is of continuing significance. The post-resurrection convert may truly know Jesus. It is perhaps not insignificant that the common emphasis in the synoptic tradition finds explicit statement in John's gospel. After showing himself to Thomas who in turn confesses belief in him, Jesus says to Thomas, 'Have you believed because you have seen me? Blessed are those who have not seen and yet believe.' (John 20:29, RSV.)

This theme that links the resurrection of Jesus and the universal mission means that Christianity must always be a universal faith. Mission is thus a continuing imperative for the Christian as he works out the terms of Jesus' death and resurrection in his own life today. It also means that there can be no Jew–Gentile division in Christianity, or any modern replacement of that kind of division; social, economic, cultic, racial, political or any other kind of division can never be tolerated by a Christian.

10

WATER TURNED INTO WINE AT CANA

John 2:1–12

We come now to five cases where we need to interpret the supernatural in John's gospel. Here we are in a different situation from the consideration of the synoptics in that John manifestly represents a tradition which stands apart from the other three gospels. The interpretation of the fourth gospel has been, and still is a matter of great debate. We are bound to consider similarities with the synoptic gospels, but they are not always there, and not always so helpful. Our method, however, is basically the same, in that we shall seek to identify the tradition which John has available to him, and to see how

112

he has interpreted that tradition. His work as an evangelist can be seen in the overall structure of the gospel, in the closer details of the various sections of the gospel and also the particular details of each story.

With the wedding at Cana we come to an incident which is obviously of great importance to John, but which seems somewhat trivial in its own right. Compared to the human needs which are the subject of other miracle stories this one seems a little out of place. It is true that joy and festivity were important elements in Jewish life, and also for Jesus, and it may be true that the dilemma of the host might have involved him not only in social embarrassment but also in financial danger, because of principles of social obligation to those who have presented gifts at the wedding. Even so, the story does seem a little insignificant in its own right. It was probably preserved by those who were involved (Jesus' family, the disciples and the families of the wedding) and it was probably preserved at Cana. The point of the story considered on its own is the excellence of what Jesus did (John 2:10) and the secrecy of the miraculous source of the wine (John 2:9); it is only members of the household who know about it.

The story of the wedding at Cana is placed in a prominent position in the overall structure of John's gospel. It is connected with the events recorded in the previous chapter by the time note with which the story begins – 'on the third day'. Aside from the prologue in chapter 1, the only narrative to come before the story of the marriage at Cana is concerned with the ministry of John the Baptist and the calling of some of the disciples. John's ministry in this section consists chiefly in testifying to Jesus, that he is the Lamb of God. Two of John's disciples hearing this testimony follow Jesus and seek instruction from him as a rabbi. This leads on to other disciples coming after Jesus, and finally Nathanael is called. All these events are located by John in the south in the vicinity of Bethany, and they reflect the Jewish location of John's ministry and of the first disciples of Jesus. The calling of the disciples is completed here with the calling of Nathanael who particularly is said to be an Israelite in whom there is no guile. The first chapter is formed in the heart of Judaism, but the second chapter of John's gospel steps out into the atmosphere of the Galilee of the Gentiles.

John sees considerable significance in the various journeys made by Jesus from Galilee to Judaea, and in particular to Jerusalem. Cana is a Galilean stop-over in the first journey from the south to the northern base of Jesus' ministry in Capernaum. Its prominent position in the structure of the gospel points to the transition that is being made from Judaea to Galilee, from Israel to the nations. A new beginning is being made; Judaism is being replaced.

In the more particular details of the context of this story, we note first that this is a remarkable sign in that it is not the basis for a discourse, as for example the feeding of the five thousand in John 6 is the basis for the long discourse on the bread of life. The point of the story is thus to be found not in lengthy explication but in the very terms of the story, and the clues which John gives as he tells it.

There are a number of striking clues as to the way in which John is interpreting this story. We can list them so that the direction in which they point is more clear.

1. He notes that the story is located in Cana in Galilee. He does this at the beginning of the story in verse 1, and in the summary at the end of the story in verse 11.

2. The very material which is changed in the miracle is signalled as being there for the Jewish rites of purification. The new wine of the Kingdom is made from the water of Judaism.

3. The miracle is a 'sign', that is to say something which shows forth Jesus as the Messiah sent by God.

4. The 'hour' is not yet, but it is brought near by the very doing of this sign. The sign anticipates and points forward to the hour of Jesus' death (see John 7:30; 8:20; 12:23).

5. The sign is a manifestation of Jesus' glory. This does not mean his gloriousness or magnificence, but rather his true character and mission. John thinks of Jesus as being sent to reveal the Father, or to reveal his glory. He is sent to reveal God's presence and power. For John that presence and power is chiefly revealed in Jesus' hour, that is to say at the crucifixion.

6. The effect of the story is that the disciples believed in him. So far in John's gospel the disciples have only come to the conclusion that Jesus is the Messiah; John has not so far said that they believed in him. The last section dealing with the calling of the disciples in John 1:51 clearly indicates that the disciples so far have only a very meagre understanding; indeed that they believe is actually questioned in John 1:50.

114

These clues point in the same direction as the indication given by the place of this story in the gospel as a whole and by the details of the closer context of the story. John, by the way in which he has told this story, interprets it as a sign of the new beginning in Jesus. That new beginning involves the replacement of Judaism, but a replacement which arises from within Judaism itself.

It is very important to note that the same trend away from the 'marvellous' as we found in the synoptic gospels is also shown by John. However, John directs his interpretation less specifically to the ethical and more particularly to belief in Jesus as the revelation of the glory of the Father.

This interpretative direction sets the line of emphasis for the Christian today. The completeness of the revelation of the Father in Jesus gives a focus for his faith. In two respects this is important. First Christianity is not and can never be a national religion, nor can it be localized in one particular cultural expression. Christianity must always be a universal faith which cuts across all national, cultural, geographical and historical barriers. Secondly the one test for true Christian faith is its continuity with Jesus of Nazareth. John focuses very closely on Jesus, but at the same time is acutely aware of those who come to believe in him after the historical life of the man.

John thinks of the Christian believer of later generations as knowing Jesus through the Spirit. The Spirit is the one who replaces the human presence of Jesus. In this way John is able to grapple with the situation of the modern Christian. How can modern man know Jesus of Nazareth in his own modern world? John's answer, in his 'later' day, is through the Spirit. However, he is careful to point out that the Spirit testifies to Jesus, and therefore the place of Jesus of Nazareth is preserved. What John has done is to vindicate the religious experience of man when that experience is interpreted according to the Jesus model. Modern man (according to this pattern) is to take his religious experience and interpret and direct it according to the pattern and teaching of Jesus of Nazareth. The idea of religionless Christianity – in the sense of Christianity without religious experience – is thus a distortion.

11

THE WOMAN OF SAMARIA

John 4:1–42

The story of the woman of Samaria and her conversation with Jesus figures large in the popular Christian imagination, probably because of the skill with which the story is told, and because of its intimate biographical character. In this respect it is like the immediately preceding story of Jesus' conversation with Nicodemus. The story of the woman, however, was probably kept alive in the first instance for quite different reasons. It is really the tradition of the beginning of the Christian group in the otherwise almost unknown village of Sychar. Presumably a woman had been among the first converts, and the group looked back to her conversion as the starting point of the life of the group. Her conversion was particularly memorable because it involved a personal meeting with Jesus himself in which he showed remarkable – indeed supernatural – knowledge of the woman's personal life. We are dealing with a tradition kept alive at Sychar because of its importance to them.

John has given this simple origin story a wider significance in his gospel. He places the story in a section of the gospel which is about the replacement of Judaism. This section has begun with the first sign at Cana in Galilee, and ends with the second sign done from Cana (for an official's sick servant who was in fact some distance away in Capernaum). In between these two signs Jesus has been to Jerusalem where he cleared out the temple and declared he would raise up a new temple. In Jerusalem he had also been engaged in theological discourse by a leader of Judaism. That leader, Nicodemus, has no real knowledge of God, and Jesus teaches him about the new birth. Having shown Jesus as superior to Judaism in Judaea, John now provides an intermediate story which takes the narrative from Judaean Judaism to Galilee of the Gentiles. This intermediate story is followed by a miracle done in Galilee for a Gentile family. Just as the disciples believed in Jesus as a result of the first sign in Cana, so this man's family also believe in Jesus as a result of the second sign done in Cana.

In the closer context of the story this intermediate (or transpositional) function of the story can be seen in the elaborate geographical note with which John introduces the story. Jesus was really intent on going from Judaea to Galilee, but he had to go through

Samaria. That fact enabled John to locate the story of the origin of the Sychar Christian group in his narrative. He does so in such a way that the theme he is intent on developing is highlighted.

As with the story of the wedding at Cana John has indicated his interpretative line by a number of signals or clues in the details of the story. Unlike his account of the miracle of the water turned into wine, John has developed an emphasis and a balance in the story which also reflect his interpretative interests. First of all, the clues in the story:

1. The conversation with the woman is located not actually in the town but on the site of Jacob's well. The location and the actual well, which went so far back into the tradition of Judaism, are used to illustrate the replacement of Judaism.

2. The Samaritan challenge to Jerusalem-based Judaism is picked up, again by reference to the location near Shechem, in order to be rejected. It is to be rejected because it is not the true replacement of Judaism.

3. The remarkable insight which Jesus has is turned into a definition of the Messiah. But the Jews did not in fact expect to be taught all things by the Messiah. They expected in the last days to be taught by God. There was some expectation that the nations, and perhaps the Jews in the dispersion, would be taught the commandments by the Messiah, but not 'all things'. John has turned his tradition about the conversion of this woman in a more specifically messianic direction, so that this conversion by 'marvel' has become a conversion by the fulfilment of prophetic expectation about the Messiah of Judaism.

4. The testimony of the woman, in the first instance so important in her conversion, is in the end discounted by the people of Sychar. They come to believe because of the word that Jesus has spoken to them. The conclusion here is the same as that expressed by the disciples at the end of the long discourse on the bread of life in John 6: 'you have the words of eternal life.'

5. At the end of the story the people of Sychar come to believe that Jesus is the saviour of the world. Jesus' salvation thus comprehends all men; it is universal, not national.

All these clues point to John's theme: Jesus is the saviour of the world and belief in him replaces Judaism. They also show John dramatically discounting the supernatural insight of Jesus as a basis for belief in him. He does not deny that there is a kind of belief which can arise from this, but it is clearly not the belief which his gospel is seeking to bring. John has also changed the emphasis of the story, by the extended discourse on living water which precedes the 'marvellous' conversion of the woman. That discourse, so closely integrated into the details of the event, precisely expresses his thematic interest and the direction of his interpretation.

Even though it is a very different form of the supernatural from that in the miracle of the water changed into wine at Cana, John's control of his material according to his own interpretative intentions means that the story is moved in much the same direction as the wedding story. Thus the completeness of the revelation of the Father in Jesus is the key issue. The universality of the faith, the impossibility of its restriction to national, geographical or cultural bounds—these are implications of John's systematic interpretation of Jesus' supernatural insight in this story.

There is one extra point in this story that was not apparent in the story of the marriage at Cana. Here John clearly indicates that the abiding significance of Jesus for the people of Sychar, as they contemplate belief in Jesus without his continuing physical presence with them, is the word which they have heard from him. It is true that in one sense Jesus is himself that word, but it is also true that the word which Jesus brings is able to be expressed and formulated. John's portrayal of Jesus giving long discourses shows this. It is especially clear in the extended farewell discourses which anticipate the time when Jesus will not be present in the same physical way. Thus for the modern Christian the teaching of Jesus becomes an important resource in his understanding of the terms of his commitment to Christ.

John has all but eliminated the supernatural from the tradition which he had received, not by denying it, but by pointing away from it to far more important and more abiding things. If the modern Christian is to follow the line suggested by John's interpretation of the supernatural then he will similarly not deny it, in this 'marvellous' form, but he will not point to it as in any sense central. He will direct his attention to the far more important and fundamental matters of Jesus and his word.

12

JESUS WALKS ON THE SEA

John 6: 16–21 (Matthew 14: 22–33; Mark 6: 45–52)

The account of Jesus walking on the sea to his disciples brings us to a different interpretative task, in that this story is almost certainly about the same incident as that recorded in Matthew and Mark. The three accounts have the incident immediately following a feeding miracle, and there are a number of parallels between them. So we have not only to consider the characteristic Johannine method of working in discerning the interpretation of the event, but we are also able to take into account the synoptic differences.

Lying behind these accounts is the tradition of Jesus walking to his disciples across the sea. They had gone ahead of him, for some reason or other, and were finding the going difficult because of wind and rough seas. At this critical point Jesus turns up. Since we are principally concerned with John's interpretation of this story we shall concentrate on the points of comparison which help to draw it out.

First of all we should note the general place of this story in the gospel. It is clearly part of the extended discourse in John on the bread of life which is built on the feeding miracle told in 6: 1–15. This is the first major discourse to a crowd in John and is followed by a number of such discourses. The story of the lake crossing enables John to bring Jesus back to Capernaum where he knows the discourse on the bread of life was held. In this sense the walking on the lake has an important structural role in John's gospel. It advances the theme of Jesus as the bread of life. Mark connects the walking on the lake with the feeding miracle also, but only by way of allusion in order to explain the disciples' unbelief. In John, however, they are portrayed as believing; they are glad when Jesus comes into the boat. Furthermore at the end of the discourse on the bread of life which follows, the disciples are again portrayed as believing in Jesus. In contrast to those disciples who no longer followed him Peter answers for the twelve, 'Lord, to whom shall we go? You have the words of eternal life; and we have believed, and come to know, that you are the Holy One of God.' (John 6: 68, RSV.)

As with the previous Johannine examples we have considered, the various clues to John's interpretation of this supernatural event can be simply listed, together with the comparative points from the synoptic accounts.

1. In John it is already evening when the disciples set off in the boat, and when Jesus comes to them it is dark. Mark and Matthew give the time (the fourth watch) but John is more interested in simply noting that it was dark and that it was night. Quite apart from the contrasting imagery of light which is so important to John, night and darkness are suggestive of evil for him.

2. John does not say that the disciples thought Jesus was a ghost as Matthew and Mark do. John's account is much less dramatic and his portrayal of the disciples much more favourable.

3. All three gospels record that Jesus says to the disciples, 'It is I, do not be afraid'. This translation disguises a little that the words actually used are 'I am' and, while these words do not have highly distinctive associations in Matthew or Mark, they do in John. In the discourse on the bread of life of which this walking on the lake incident is a part, we have the first of the great 'I am' sayings of John's gospel: *I am* the bread of life (6:35); the light of the world (8:12); the door of the sheep (10:7); the good shepherd (10:11); the resurrection and the life (11:25); the way, the truth, and the life (14:6); and the true vine (15:1). Jesus had also used these words to disclose his true identity to the woman of Samaria (4:26), and it is almost certain that here (in John 6) John understands these words in terms of his use of them elsewhere.

4. John alone notes that when Jesus had come into the boat they then came to the land to which they were going.

There are a number of clues here to John's interpretation of this supernatural story in terms of his own themes and interests. However, there is no great amount of evidence of a thoroughgoing attempt by John to integrate this story into his own conceptions of Christ. Rather the story seems to fulfil the simple structural point of leading on to the discourse on the bread of life. When the crowd seeks to enquire about the way by which Jesus had got across the lake he simply cuts across their question and takes them back to the feeding and on to the bread of life discourse. This is in contrast to the wedding at Cana and the insight into the private life of the woman of Samaria by Jesus.

Did John fail to recast and interpret the story of Jesus walking on the lake because he felt it could stand in his gospel perfectly adequately as it was? Or did he simply take it and use it for the structural purpose that we have already noted? I think that he was content with the story – he is far too systematic in his writing to have left such an undigested lump in his narrative. That means that the idea of Jesus simply walking on the water in the way described was acceptable to him. It is true that by stretching things a little you could argue that he intended his readers to understand that Jesus had simply walked a little way into the water, and was really walking alongside the lake. Even so, although he does tell the story less vividly than Matthew and Mark, he surely intends us to understand Jesus as doing something quite supernatural.

This story presents the modern Christian with a great problem, for he finds it difficult to understand how God allows irregularities to occur in the way natural things happen. The problem is that the supernatural in this story is just there and accepted as part of the passing scene. The modern person might be somewhat suspicious if he had a story which was an obvious wonder-worker story, since Jesus seems to have shunned such attitudes – a thing with which the modern man can identify.

It is not much help to note that the story has only Jesus walking on the lake (in Matthew Peter goes across the water to meet Jesus) since John makes no attempt to restrict such things to Jesus. The problem is the lack of an interpretative line which would lead us in some direction or other. It is clear that John does not focus on the incident, and in that sense he implies that it is not as important as the other things in the context upon which he does focus. But what do we say to such events today? Do we claim that they could not have happened, and that they are to be regarded as the invention of the early Christians? That is one way to deal with the problem, but it hardly carries any conviction on simple historical grounds.

To say that from an historical point of view it seems that this thing did in fact happen, is not to say that it could or should be repeated. The most that it says is that, in principle, the Christian cannot rule out the possibility of its happening again. If it does, then the Christian is bound, following John (and the trend of the New Testament as a whole), to take it in his stride and not to make a wonder out of it. This brings us to the heart of the whole question. Supernatural events are clearly possible in the Christian understanding, but they are just as odd for the Christian to understand as they are for any other person. The Christian has as his focus earthly commitment to his fellow man, and this as the expression of his commitment to Jesus. The idea of being heavenly minded or wrapped up in the supernatural in such a way that the love of his neighbour falls from the central focus of his life and action is certainly not in accord with New Testament Christianity. For the modern Christian, then, this story of Jesus walking on the lake implies what we could call a take-it-or-leave-it attitude to the so-called supernatural which he encounters today.

13

LAZARUS RAISED FROM THE DEAD

John 11:1–44

This is undoubtedly the most dramatic and striking of the miracles in John's gospel. There is no parallel in the other gospels, so we have here a story based on John's own tradition. Some have suggested that the parable in Luke 16:19–31 about the rich man and Lazarus might be the basis from which the story grew. However there is not really much in common between these two stories and they are quite unrelated. The story considered as part of the tradition John was dealing with is really a portent and sign of Jesus' authority. The story demonstrates the truth of John 5:21 that 'as the Father raises the dead and gives them life, so also the Son gives life to whom he will' (RSV).

In the overall structure of John's gospel this story is an important pointer to the imminent death of Jesus. It is the direct occasion for the Jews to plot his death (John 11:53). It is also the last sign in the first half of the gospel, if not in the gospel as a whole, and the immediately following paragraph provides a link between this story and the end of the first part of the gospel. It is therefore the climax of the first part of the gospel, and a pointer to the passion with which the second half of the gospel is preoccupied.

There are two important details in the immediate context which are pointers to John's understanding of this story. At the end of the previous section John gives us a summary of the effect of Jesus' teaching on the Jews. He records that many believed in Jesus and saw him as fulfilling what John had said about him. However the summary at the end of the Lazarus story, while containing a reference to the many that believed in Jesus, also records that some went to the chief priests and Pharisees, and this in turn leads on to the resolution of the Jewish authorities to kill Jesus.

The second pointer in the context is the identification, at the beginning of the Lazarus story, of Mary as the one who had anointed Jesus (John 11:2). When this story is told in John 12 Jesus clearly interprets her action as an anointing for his death. In other words, in the context we find two clues about John's interpretation of this story and they both point in the direction of Jesus' imminent death.

In the story itself there are a number of clues which show how John understands this story. Unlike some of the other stories in John's gospel the interpretative clues in this narrative do not all point in the same direction. Nevertheless, they show how, at this critical point in his gospel, John is preparing his reader for what is to follow.

1. When Jesus announced to his disciples that he would go back into Judaea they warned him that the Jews there wanted to stone him. However, they agreed to go with him, and Thomas expressed the point by saying, 'let us also go that we may die with him'. John understands that this last venture into Judaea will lead to Jesus' death.

2. The plot against Jesus comes from the Jews. Normally John means by this the Jewish authorities, and stoning was the official means of execution for blasphemy. However in John 10:31 it seems more like mob lynching, though the result of the Lazarus story is to make the plot more precisely official. In John 11:53 it is the chief priests and Pharisees who plot to kill Jesus; during the Lazarus story the death of Jesus has become official policy.

3. The narrative is anticipated and explained in the discourse between Jesus and the two sisters. This contrasts with John 6 where the miracle is interpreted after the event in a long discourse. First Martha goes to Jesus expressing the hopes of his healing her brother. Jesus reassures her that Lazarus will rise again, but Martha understands that in terms of the final general resurrection which, as a Jew, she believes in. Jesus without again referring to Lazarus tells her that he Jesus, in his own person, brings that final resurrection into the present. He is the resurrection and the life, and participation in that final resurrection is by belief in Jesus. Martha says that she believes this, and that she believes that Jesus is the Christ, the Son of God, he who is coming into the world. This is the Christian confession. She does not at this point specifically relate this to her brother Lazarus, and when Jesus later tells them to roll the stone away she objects that there will be a stink. This discourse points to resurrection and life, yet

it is remarkable how little the Johannine terms for resurrection and life are used in the chapter. The point here is that the resurrection and life are to be found in Jesus. He anticipates the last times, and he calls men to believe in him that they might share in that end-time resurrection and life now.

4. In John 11:9 Jesus tells the disciples that if anyone walks in the day he does not stumble, because he sees the light of this world. Here he touches on the idea of light and darkness, which is so important to John as a contrast image for good and evil. The point is much the same as that in John 12:35, namely that the time of the presence of Jesus as the light is coming to an end. We are moving to the conclusion of Jesus' ministry.

5. Another important term in John is 'glory'. At the beginning of this story Jesus says that Lazarus' illness is not unto death, but is for the glory of God so that the Son of God might be glorified by it. Then at the very point of the raising of Lazarus Jesus tells Martha that if she believes she will see the glory of God. This term illustrates the two-sided character of the story as a whole. On the one hand, glory here points to resurrection, yet in the following chapters of John's gospel we will see more clearly that the Son of God is principally glorified in his death.

6. Just before Lazarus is called out of his grave Jesus gives voice to a prayer. It is unusual enough for Jesus to pray in public like this, but in the prayer he actually says that he does not need to pray thus, but he does so for the sake of the other people present. It is a rather self-conscious declaration of the unity between the Father and the Son. That intimate unity is very important to John's gospel. Jesus is sent by the Father, will return to the Father and lives in continual fellowship with the Father. Thus for John, the signs which Jesus does are also the works of the Father.

The obvious point of this story, as far as John is concerned, is that Jesus is the resurrection and the life, that he brings in his own person the reality of the final resurrection which can be experienced by those who believe in him. The story also brings to a climax the ministry of Jesus thus far, and clearly points on to the end of the ministry in Jesus' death. There is also the hint that his death is the true moment of the glorification of the Son of God. This means that what appears to be defeat is in reality triumph. When the Son is lifted up on the cross he will draw all men to himself.

This story brings us to the heart of Christian faith in a way that is matched only by the story of Jesus' own resurrection. It contains the seeds of the view that the crucifixion is the great triumph, and that all signs of God's power and glory are to be understood in these terms; thus the challenge of Paul that human wisdom and signs have nothing to do with the Christian proclamation. That power really resides in the proclamation of the cross. All true greatness consists in service and giving oneself up for ones fellows. In other words, true reality is not that which belongs to this world. It belongs outside this world, and those who participate in this reality have ceased to belong to this world. The demonstration of this power is therefore in terms which this world normally accounts the opposite of power and glory, such as suffering, humility and death.

There is a strong tradition of such thinking in Christian history and it has often been regarded as making a great divide between this world and God. Yet there is also another tradition in Christian thought. This affirms that the power of God is identifiable in this world in terms which are not necessarily the opposite of those which normally apply. According to the first tradition of thought Lazarus' death is not a sign of the failure of God's power or glory, and like other deaths should be left. However, John says that Lazarus is raised from the dead to the glory of God, thus reflecting our second tradition of thought. The story tradition with which John is working views the raising of Lazarus almost entirely in these terms.

We can press the point further by asking what would have happened when Lazarus finally died. His fellow Christians would have buried him in the hope of his participation in the final resurrection. In Paul's terms he would have been among the dead in Christ, and would be raised first at Christ's return. In other words, as far as Lazarus himself was concerned his raising by Jesus after his first death was a very considerable irregularity, not only from the point of view of a medical scientist, but also from the point of view of Christian understanding. It is as hard for Christian theology to digest the story of the raising of Lazarus as it is for the so-called scientific mind.

This is in fact the real significance of the Lazarus story for the Christian today. It is an irregularity which prepares the way for Jesus' death as a triumph and a glory. The Christian is committed to two 'incarnations', and one of these involves the belief that God has revealed himself in the person of the man Jesus. Such a communications effort necessarily involves concessionary language, such as a scientist might use in explaining black holes to a layman. In such a situation the incarnation of Jesus can never be completely convincing. It is always a matter of belief. The Lazarus story, by its very irregularity, points to the uniqueness of this incarnation.

The Christian is someone who believes in Jesus, that is, he commits himself to Jesus as being from the Father. Thus his commitment implies a further incarnation, the incarnation of the Son of God in the life of the Christian. Jesus' call to follow him points to this, just as does John's insistence that the disciple will receive the same treatment from the world as Jesus did. The farewell discourses in John's gospel are a preparation of the disciples for the time when they will embody the word of God.

14

A VOICE ASSURES JESUS

John 12:27–36

There is no parallel in the other gospels to this story of Jesus being encouraged in prayer by a voice from heaven. There is a voice from heaven at the transfiguration and Jesus spends time in prayer in the garden of Gethsemane in the other gospels, but these accounts are so different from what we have here in John that it is difficult to think they are related. There is, of course, no transfiguration in John, and no prayer in the garden of Gethsemane. We are therefore dealing with a piece of tradition known only to John.

This story comes at a critical place in the development of John's gospel. It comes in the sayings which were prompted by the arrival of the Greeks in Jerusalem for the feast, who asked to see Jesus (John 12:20ff.). It comes immediately before the conclusion of the first half of the gospel. The second half of the gospel advances the narrative very little in terms of Jesus' public ministry since it is taken up with Jesus' farewell discourses with his disciples. In this way the sayings prompted by the arrival of the Greeks, including this story of the voice from heaven, come right at the end of John's account of Jesus' ministry.

A number of details in the immediate context point to the story's looking forward to the passion narrative from the perspective of the completion of the public ministry. Jesus' answer to the enquiry of the

Greeks is that the hour has come for the Son of Man to be glorified; and then he goes on, unless a grain of wheat falls into the earth and dies it remains alone – but if it dies it bears much fruit. This last phrase 'bears much fruit' anticipates John 15:1–8 where the image is applied to the disciples. At the end of the paragraph in 12:36b John tells us that Jesus hid himself from them, clearly showing that his public ministry is at an end.

The context of the story is therefore the end of the public ministry and the anticipation of the impending death of Jesus. Jesus' prayer first of all shows his human shrinking from this impending death, but also the (similarly human) faith which accepts the purpose of his life. The purpose of his life is that he should come to this 'hour', and be glorified in it by his own death. The voice assures Jesus that the Father's name has already been glorified (in the life of obedience which has brought Jesus to this hour) and it will be glorified again (in the death of the obedient servant Jesus). As far as Jesus is concerned the voice means that even – or especially – at this hour of greatest trial he is still in the closest union with the Father.

While the voice may bring encouragement to Jesus, it brings judgement to those who hear it. The response to the voice, which Jesus says has come for the sake of those who heard it, divides the hearers. Some ascribe it to an angel, while others of a more mundane mentality regard it as thunder. Whether they actually heard thunder, which some regarded as an angel's voice, or whether they actually heard a voice, which some refused to accept (or 'hear'), we cannot say. What we can say is that they heard what they were prepared to believe, a thing which is true of all hearing. The voice is not referred to again, and its principal function in the narrative is to raise and highlight the question of judgement.

John clearly thinks of this voice as the voice of the Father. The response of men to the word of God is the sign of their judgement. In the wider picture of the gospel, the word of God is Jesus himself and his coming brings judgement in the sense that men are divided by his coming. Those who hear and believe become the sons of light, and those who do not hear and do not believe show that they are sons of darkness. John's interpretation of the voice event means that the hearing of God's word is of critical importance to man. He is to attend to Jesus and to follow him. Jesus thus becomes the touchstone by which judgement and belief are to be identified.

If Jesus becomes the touchstone in this way then the Christian can adopt a more balanced attitude to the unusual, and what is customarily called the supernatural. He is prepared to see or hear the unusual. Where the unusual (or for that matter the usual) indicates to him something about the meaning of his life and the way he lives that life, then he can measure it against Jesus. Where there is conflict he can be sure that what is out of line with Jesus is fraudulent. Yet where the usual or the unusual speaks with the voice of Jesus then he responds to this as the voice of God. The testing of all things, especially ethical norms and decisions, by the standard of Jesus raises the most basic question for the modern Christian: who is Jesus Christ? It is very significant that the question is raised for us by a passage which comes at the end of an account of the public ministry of Jesus. That fact emphasizes to us the commitment of Christians in every age to Jesus of Nazareth, to the historical Jesus.

Christianity is torn by two commitments. On the one hand it is completely committed to a set of historical events set in Palestine in the first century. The quest for the historical Jesus is a natural expression of that commitment. On the other hand Christianity is committed to the reality of the present and contemporary experience of God, and specifically to a life of committed love for the rest of creation. At a time when religion tends to be experiential, and the odd is sometimes thought to have greater claim to divine origin than the ordinary, it is worth emphasizing commitment to the public knowledge of Jesus. Such public knowledge can and must be both historical – even antiquarian – and contemporary. People often hear voices. The particular voice which John writes about points to Jesus as the one in whom God has been glorified in his public ministry, and in whom God will be glorified in his public death.

15

THE PENTECOST PHENOMENON

Acts 2:1–42 (10:44–48; 11:15ff.; 19:6)

In the Acts of the Apostles we have to use a slightly different method in order to understand the way in which Luke is interpreting the supernatural things which he records. This is because his way of writing is different from John's, and because his is the only source we have for the material we are considering. It is certain that Luke had various sources available to him when he was writing, but it is extremely difficult to identify these sources with any certainty. If we could, then we would be in a better position to see how Luke has used and interpreted them. The literary structure of Acts is Luke's work, and we should therefore take that into account in considering any given story of the supernatural. Luke tends not to use 'clue words' as John does. He tends rather to provide some kind of explanation for what he regards as important, by means of either a sermon or a narrative told in a particular way.

The event that lies behind the story of the first day of Pentecost clearly relates to the beginning of the Christian preaching in Jerusalem, and to the development of a Christian group which was more open and public in its activities than had been the case with the disciples and their friends after Jesus' resurrection. It also clearly has to do with the experience of the apostles in prompting them to commence preaching. It is worth observing that only on the day of Pentecost does this strange phenomenon receive any explanation. The two later references to something similar in Samaria (Acts 10 and 11) and Asia (Acts 19) are regarded by Luke as shadows of the original. The Acts 2 story is the fundamental event in terms of the general structure of Acts. The interpretation given to the event confirms this view.

The setting of the story is carefully prepared by Luke. First the risen Jesus discourses at length with the disciples about the Kingdom, and the restoration of the Kingdom is pointed to by the disciples' question. The full number of the twelve is made up by the election of Matthias. Never before, and never again, was the presence of the full number of the twelve thought to be of such importance. The disciples are waiting in the city to receive the promise of the Father, according to Jesus' instructions.

The strange sound of wind, the appearance of tongues of fire are not the significant things as far as the onlookers are concerned. What strikes them is the fact that they can hear these Christians declaring the mighty works of God in their own different languages. A great crowd of people, mostly Jews or proselytes who had come up for the festival, are then given an explanation of this strange event by Peter's sermon. Peter addresses his sermon first of all to 'men of Judaea and all who dwell in Jerusalem' (Acts 2:14), then more generally 'men of Israel' (2:22), and more intimately 'brethren' (2:29). The peroration is addressed to 'all the house of Israel'. Peter has in mind a Jewish audience, and his argument appeals to what would be persuasive to a Jewish audience – the Old Testament – and an argument relating to King David.

The argument of this sermon is simple and clear. First Peter declares that this is not drunkenness but the fulfilment of the prophecy of Joel about the last days. The strange speaking in foreign languages by these Jews is a sign of the last days (see Joel 2:28–32; Isaiah 32:15; 44:3; Ezekiel 39:29). Having made this point about the evidence before his audience, Peter then goes back to Jesus and declares that he was attested to by signs and wonders from God, that according to God's plan he was killed, and by God he was raised from the dead. These assertions are supported by a quotation from Psalm 16:8–11 which, if read in a particular way, refers to David being raised from the dead. Peter takes the Psalm in this way, and then asserts that David is dead and did not rise from the dead; his tomb is still here to see. The Psalm should be understood as a prophecy referring to the Christ. At this point (Acts 2:32) Peter goes back to his second claim, that Jesus was raised from the dead by God. The conclusion is clear – Jesus is the Christ, the true Son of David.

Having thus established that Jesus is the Davidic Messiah, Peter then goes on to connect this with the point he had started with. Jesus as the Davidic Messiah has been raised from the dead, and has now been exalted to the right hand of God. This also could not refer to David, since David anticipated that his Lord would occupy this exalted position. The pouring out of the Spirit is the evidence of Jesus' reception at the right hand of God after his ascension. Therefore, the evidence now before his hearers is the final proof of Jesus' ascension to the throne of David: he is Lord and Christ.

This argument has more point when it is remembered that the Old Testament prophecies about the outpouring of the Spirit in the last days are associated with the restoration of the Davidic kingdom. Peter uses arguments based on the signs of Jesus, the supernatural phenomenon before his hearers, and the witness of the disciples to Jesus' resurrection. These points are used in conjunction with quotations from Joel and the Psalms. The point of interest for us is that the argument is a once for all argument. It is intended to show that Jesus has fulfilled the 'end days' prophecy of Joel, that he is the Messiah, the exalted King of Israel who has now ascended to the throne of David. The kingdom, thus restored, can move out from

Jerusalem, and when significant boundaries are crossed a shadow of this sign is repeated. This happens only in terms of the witnessing mission.

The meaning of this passage today is of contemporary interest in that we have recently seen a resurgence of renewal amongst Christians, which some refer to as pentecostal. By so doing they usually mean that the events of the day of Pentecost are (and should be) repeating themselves in this renewal. Luke does not think of the Pentecost phenomenon as speaking in tongues, but as the ability to speak clearly in a foreign language so that a listener hears clearly in his own tongue about the mighty acts of God. Furthermore Luke, by the way Peter's interpretation is set out, clearly believes that this is a particular historical event related to Jesus' ascension and designation as king over the restored kingdom of David. It is something of an irony that Luke's own interpretation of the events on the day of Pentecost shows that he could never have been or called himself a Pentecostal.

The significance for the modern Christian lies in the fact that this event, according to Luke's interpretation, is one of the historical foundation events of Christianity. It belongs in the past. It speaks to the present in so far as it points to two fundamental things. First that Christianity grew out of Judaism, and has inherited from Judaism an understanding of God and his will for men which must inform the reading of the New Testament. Secondly that the central point in Christianity is the confession that Jesus is Lord.

16

HEALING A LAME MAN AT THE GATE BEAUTIFUL

Acts 3:1–4:31

There are some points of similarity in the form of this story to that of the raising of Lazarus in John's gospel. First there is a dramatic healing which is observed by a large number of people. This is the occasion of a discourse, and then of opposition from the Jewish authorities. Here Peter and John on their way into the temple heal a man in the name of Jesus Christ of Nazareth and this provides the occasion for a sermon. In this respect the story is very characteristic of Acts, and similar to the story of the day of Pentecost. Unlike the

Pentecost story this miracle is not regarded by Luke as a once only event. It is not bound into the fabric of the event of Jesus' incarnation.

The sermon which Peter gives is not easy to follow exactly, or consistently. This may be due to some mixing of the sources which Luke had available to him. However, the main thrust of the sermon is clear enough. First of all he identifies the author of the miracle as the God of the Jews (the God of Abraham, Isaac and Jacob, the God of our Fathers) – 'that same God glorified Jesus whom you killed, but whom God raised up'. He next claims the witness of the disciples to Jesus' resurrection and the witness of the healing of the lame man as having been done through faith in Jesus. He then appeals to the prophets to show that the Christ must suffer, as indeed Jesus had done, and to the heritage and role of the Jews as sons of the covenant. The main thrust of the argument is apologetic. Peter is trying to convert his hearers to belief in Jesus. The miracle is a piece of manifest evidence if he can make the connexion between it and Jesus. Having done that in the opening part of the sermon, he then goes on to more general Jewish apologetic arguments.

In the confrontation with the Jewish authorities, Peter first of all gives his basic Christian confession that the miracle had been done through the name of Jesus Christ of Nazareth. He asserts that Jesus is the stone rejected by the builders, but now become the head of the corner. This is a reference to Psalm 118:22, which the Jews had variously related to Abraham, David or the Messiah. The healing of the lame man is now regarded even by the Jewish authorities as a 'notable sign' (Acts 4:16). The question for them is how far the healing will be regarded by people in Jerusalem as a sign of God's confirmation of the preaching of the Christians.

So from Luke's point of view the healing of this lame man is not a unique historical event, but simply an occasion for preaching the gospel. The appeal to the healing as part of the apologetic in Peter's sermon is not very great, and certainly not as significant to him as the appeal to the fulfilment of the Old Testament. The evidence for the fulfilment of the Old Testament by Jesus is argued on the basis of the resurrection of Jesus, to which the disciples are witnesses, and on the basis of Jesus' conformity to the expectation that the Messiah would suffer.

Clearly the focus in this story is on the great salvation events of Jesus' life, death and resurrection. This must be the perspective for

132

any thinking by modern Christians. The demand which Peter makes at the end of his sermon is that they should repent and believe. Faith in Jesus and commitment to his way are the central points. That is what is significant. Furthermore the actual healing of the man is Peter's expression of that way of Jesus, his compassion on men and provision for their needs.

The focusing on the testimony and commitment to Jesus in the way that Luke tells this story, and in the way that Peter uses the story to develop an evangelistic appeal, points to the way in which the modern Christian should deal with the story. The healing is a notable sign and belongs to the present and contemporary situation for Peter. However, he turns away from this very quickly and focuses on the past – what Jesus did and how he fulfilled Old Testament expectations. For the modern Christian this highlights the inevitable antiquarian character of his faith. His faith always has an historical perspective, looking back to the time of Jesus in Palestine. In the early church this retrospective element in the faith was present to Christians in their attention and devotion to the tradition. The apostles handed on the tradition of their teaching and preaching, and almost all sections of the New Testament show a concern for the continuation of the tradition by a process of receiving and handing on. So it is an important part of the Christianity of the New Testament that they looked back to Jesus through the tradition. The modern Christian is no less committed to this historical attitude. He looks back to Jesus through the tradition. That is the past and controlling point of reference for him. Peter's thrust is backwards to Jesus – so is ours.

Nevertheless the healing of the lame man was very much in the present, and the religious experience of the Christian today (as part of his whole experience of life) is very much part of the present. That too is a basic and essential part of the Christian position. The Christian is thus committed in two ways. On the one hand he is committed in looking back in history to Jesus, and on the other he is committed in the present to his experience of people and the world. This present, or contemporary experience is made up of things which we think of as normal and regular and things which are not so normal, but positively irregular. The healing of the man at the Gate Beautiful was just such for Peter, and there is no reason to think that such irregularities are excluded for our present experience. Clearly people do witness odd things, and we cannot explain everything in nice neat patterns.

We need to distinguish the irregular part of Peter's experience – the

healing of the lame man – from the present experience which he urged
on his hearers. He did not tell them to go and heal lame people, or to
focus their attention on such oddities. Rather he urged on them repentance. The central and important present experience which Peter
desired was moral in character. In this respect he was true to Jesus'
own emphasis and to what would become the central line of Christian
tradition. What is enjoined is not odd, esoteric or even strangely
religious, but rather it is basically moral. I am not saying that
Christianity is simply a moral code. On the contrary I am saying that
the form which commitment to Christ takes is fundamentally moral.
Religious experience, in the sense of an awareness of the holy, the
strange or what some have called the 'other' or the 'numinous', is not a
fundamental part of Christianity. It is part of the wide range of human
experience shared across the boundaries of different religions. The
different understandings of reality in those different religions is the
basis for their interpretation and use of religious experience. In this
story, and generally in the New Testament, we find that the primary
expression or manifestation of commitment to Christ is ethical. The
religious experience is taken as one of the facts of the situation, and
used to promote that more fundamental commitment to Christ which
is expressed in repentance and love of one's neighbour.

17

AN ANGEL RELEASES PETER FROM HEROD'S JAIL

Acts 12:16–19

This story is an example of supernatural intervention in the course of
events for the sake of the preaching mission, or the people engaged in
it. The event is located within the account of Herod's persecution of
the Christians and of God's judgement upon him. It also tells us of
Peter's departure to another place (Acts 12:17), which probably means
he left Jerusalem. Apart from a brief appearance at the council of
Jerusalem (Acts 15:7), he disappears from the Acts of the Apostles.

The context of the story is twofold. On the one hand it comes
within the visit of Paul and Barnabas to Jerusalem (Acts
11:30–12:25), and on the other hand it is part of Luke's description of
the judgement of Herod and his unhappy relations with the various
groupings in Palestine.

The actual story is based on a tradition about Peter's escape from prison and his departure from Jerusalem. A number of interpretative factors have helped some aspects of the tradition to be highlighted rather than others. The deliverance by an angel of the Lord is reminiscent of Acts 5:19, and of Old Testament stories where an angel of the Lord has delivered someone or Israel from trouble. It is significant that this is the last occasion in Acts when an angel of the Lord intervenes in this way, with the exception of the encouragement given to Paul by such an angel just before his shipwreck in Acts 27:23. It is a Jewish way of describing a miraculous deliverance or intervention, and in Acts such references are (with the one exception) located in Palestine.

Luke's interpretation of the story has several aspects. The main line of interpretation is that this deliverance marks the opening up of the preaching mission and the large-scale movement within the mission away from Palestine, and in particular away from Jerusalem. In the very next chapter Luke shows us that the centre for outreach is now Antioch, and the preaching mission now proceeds inevitably westwards and increasingly under the leadership of Paul. Peter, in more ways than one, is removed from the scene.

There are in addition a number of secondary themes in the story. Peter is slow to see God's hand in the deliverance he is being offered, just as he had been slow to see who Jesus was in the gospel. The prayer of the Christian group is zealous and pious, but apparently somewhat unbelieving, since they did not really expect such a direct answer to their prayers. Furthermore the Christians are persecuted by the authorities for political reasons which have nothing to do with whether or not they are law-abiding citizens. This is a theme that recurs in the rest of the Acts of the Apostles, and Luke is at pains to show the injustice of it wherever possible.

The interpretative interest which Luke reflects in this story concerns the development of the Gentile mission. That was of momentous importance to Christians in the first century, and even some time after that. However, as a movement it is of only indirect interest to the modern Christian. The movement that concerned Luke and the early church was the process of Christianity growing out of Judaism. That process too does not concern us directly today – it is completed. This does not mean that the Christian gives up the Old Testament. This is not feasible if he wishes to understand the New Testament and the historical character of God's work in Christ.

135

Less specifically, of course, Luke's interests bring before the Christian of today the challenge to preach the gospel to all creatures. The universal mission is always a challenge because it faces succeeding generations of humanity, not just extreme geographical areas. Luke's other themes in the story stand just as relevant for the modern Christian. Prayer is always an activity of faith, and the acceptance of the surprising is part of that faith. The acceptance of unjust persecution with faithfulness is a point which other New Testament writers develop more fully – for example 1 Peter. The modern Christian is still involved in that challenge. Persecution still persists. The tragedy of the modern world is that Christians are sometimes so involved in social and political situations that they do not readily see that they are part of some unjust repression or persecution.

The Christian in the western world is involved in the plight of the hungry in the developing countries. The Christians who are able to buy this book are probably more wealthy and better fed and housed than ninety per cent of humanity. The position of the western world, and of the Christians in that part of humanity, is almost a complete reversal of the persecuted minority position of the New Testament Christians. That is a situation which is relevant to the social and ethical aspects of Luke's interpretation.

18

PAUL'S UNUSUAL MIRACLES IN EPHESUS

Acts 19:11–16

The account of Paul's triumphant mission in Ephesus has an important place in the development of the story in the second half of the Acts of the Apostles. Asia was the one area that had not been successfully penetrated by the Pauline mission in Luke's picture. In Acts 16:6 we are told that the Holy Spirit prevented Paul and his associates from preaching the word in Asia, but now that last bastion falls. In Acts 19:10 Luke declares that all the residents of Asia heard the word of the Lord, both Jews and Greeks. Furthermore after these two incidents in Ephesus (the confrontation with magic and the riot of the silversmiths) Luke describes what he regards as a last triumphant tour of the Aegean area by Paul, prior to his departure for Jerusalem to pursue his destiny and go to Rome. Ephesus is Paul's last great missionary centre in the east and his success there is the crown of his work in the east. This can be seen in the extended account given by Luke of Paul's farewell to the Ephesians in chapter 20.

There are really two stories that are only told to illustrate the great success of the Ephesian mission: the burning of the books on magic and the riot of the silversmiths. Both demonstrate the tremendous impact that Paul's mission had on the pagan religious situation in Asia. On the one hand we have the great value of the books which were burned (50,000 pieces of silver) and on the other hand the impact made on the silversmiths' trade in statuettes of the goddess Diana. The story of the silversmiths' riot is for Luke the triumphant climax of Paul's mission, while the burning of the books on magic is politically less significant, although it does show Luke's concern to demonstrate the victory of the gospel over Hellenistic magic.

The central event which concerns Luke is the book burning. However, he includes the story of the sons of Sceva because it provides an occasion for the more important public event. Sceva was never a High Priest in Jerusalem, and he was probably a Jew who was some kind of pagan priestly figure. Clearly the sons of Sceva are shown as frauds by their attempt to use the name of Jesus for their magical purposes. Luke wants us to understand that the name of Jesus is more powerful than any magical charm or formula because it is the name of the risen Lord. He is more powerful than any force or power, magic included.

The summary in Acts 19:11 of the extraordinary miracles that were done through Paul is the necessary background to the story of the sons of Sceva and their attempt to imitate these miracles. The presence of the summary is demanded by the context, and we should not think that Ephesus was in this respect markedly different from other centres of Paul's mission. In 2 Corinthians 12:12 he reminds the Corinthians that the signs of a true apostle were performed among them, with signs and wonders and mighty works. However in Acts 19:11 Luke has extended the normal picture of miracles which accompany the preaching mission. Here he relates that handkerchiefs and aprons were carried away to sick people who were then healed. This is similar to the woman with the haemorrhage who touched Jesus' clothes (Mark 5:27ff.), and is something of a parallel to the story in Acts 5:15 of people carrying sick into the street to be healed by contact with Peter's shadow. Acts 19:11 is an extension of even these examples, and it is expressed very much in terms of the magic which Luke is concerned to show is inferior to the gospel. Luke has in fact incorporated magical

137

styles in describing Paul's mission in an attempt to show the victory of the gospel over these magical devices.

It is not too difficult for us to follow through Luke's interpretative line in the modern situation. He is concerned to show the superiority of the gospel over the forces of magic. This is not the magic of the entertainer in the theatre whose craft is one of sleight of hand and deftness of movement. The magic which Luke is concerned with deals with forces which seem mysterious and unknown to men. It is the sort of thing with which we are more familiar under the title of spiritism, of exorcisms and possession. These phenomena are not unknown to us today. Some people think that the way to deal with spirit possession, or demon possession, is to perform an exorcism. These 'services' are often long and dramatic in character, and those who do them often think of themselves as following Jesus' example. The problem with such activities is that they involve maximum opportunity for manipulation and great potential for serious psychological damage to those involved. The grave dangers in this area of human activity ought not to disguise the point that the gospel is still a superior power to the forces that are involved in such experiences. However, the power of the gospel is not over against God's activity in the world, but rather it is in line with it. The power of the gospel is not to be sought in terms of the odd, the peculiar and the secretive.

Because the power of the gospel is just another way of speaking about the power of God in his world, the attempt to relate that power to the odd and the unusual ought to be in line with the way God works in his world generally. Therefore exorcisms, and attempts to confront evil with the power of God, can only take place in the context of the church. The church, as a wide cross-section of humanity which is under the lordship of Christ, is the place where the true perspective of God's activity will emerge. In that perspective will be found all the understanding of God's ways of working in his world, and that includes understanding of the various branches of the human sciences, especially medicine and psychology.

19

PAUL FAILS TO DIE AFTER A SNAKE BITE

Acts 28:3-6

This story comes as Luke is approaching the climax of his Paul saga. Since the focus in Acts has shifted from Jerusalem and Palestine, Paul has emerged in the narrative as the Lucan hero. From Acts 13 onwards Paul clearly emerges as the one who is in the centre of the stage. In this hero story Paul has had a number of escapes in order that he might continue his mission and reach his goal of taking the gospel to Rome. After the triumphant tour of the Aegean area Paul journeys towards Jerusalem much in the way Jesus had journeyed there from Galilee in Luke's gospel. Once in Jerusalem he is delivered from a number of deadly threats, and he testifies to the Jews.

From this time it is apparent that Paul's destiny is not to be fulfilled in Jerusalem; he will go to Rome. He is first saved from a Jewish plot and taken to Caesarea where he is able to testify before the governor Felix and his successor Festus as well as king Agrippa. Despite a generally favourable hearing from Festus and Agrippa Paul is committed to Rome. Even during the journey Paul is the hero. A layman, he nonetheless gives accurate advice to the ship's captain about the sailing of the ship, and in the midst of the storm which led to the shipwreck he emerges as the real leader in the company. The fact that no lives were lost was due to Paul. After the stay in Malta, where they had been shipwrecked, Paul goes on his triumphant way to Rome.

In the details of the story we are examining this note of the triumphant apostle proceeding on his way to Rome is also present. It is blended in the story with the contrast between Paul as a worshipper of the true God and the natives who were grossly superstitious. Lying behind the story of the snake is the wider fact of the conversion of numbers of people on Malta, and the following story of the conversion of the leading person in the vicinity is given as evidence of this. We have then a 'hero-story', given in Luke's own style and part of his dramatic final section.

The immediate question that the modern Christian might ask of Luke's story is how far God looks after his servants in this dramatic way. That question is posed by the whole of the section in Acts from which our story is taken. The answer is that sometimes he does and sometimes he does not. Latimer and Ridley did not have the benefit of such protection, and Christians and missionaries have no great history of exemption from disease or accident. Was Paul then in a special category unlike others? Is it right to think that this kind of miraculous deliverance is reserved for the apostolic age when the gospel was establishing itself in the Roman world for the first time?

Of course, there have been some extraordinary deliverances since that time for Christians and for missionaries. But the truth is that such deliverances are remembered because they are extraordinary. This is not to say that the Christian should not look to God for deliverance. But he must recognize that such deliverance may not come his way in the particular fashion in which he wants it. People commonly expect that if some sort of deliverance comes their way on one occasion, then it may very well happen in the same way again. We sometimes, in an almost superstitious way, repeat previous patterns. An example of this can be seen in the attempt to add on to Mark's gospel an ending which is pretty clearly a superficially thought out summary of some of the things in Acts, but in Mark made into a promise from the risen Christ that such things would be a regular pattern for the Christian apostle.

The superstition of the natives of Malta in the story in Acts is stated in Luke's own terms, but superstition is still a factor in human experience today. Much ill founded belief and prejudice is mixed with many Christian ideas for some people. One only has to begin to question some of the ideas about Jesus that are held by people today to discover ill founded beliefs and superstition. This is the more strange since the gospels are open for anyone to read, and Christianity is root and branch opposed to superstition. The gospel is a matter of open and public knowledge, and may be examined by whatever means. Paul preached no secret knowledge, but by the plain statement of the truth sought to commend his gospel. Sometimes superstitions become venerated by age, and sometimes by being associated with church traditions and practices. The belief that no layman may enter the sanctuary of a church for fear of offending some religious sanctity is as silly a superstition as the belief of some Christians that things will inevitably go wrong during the day if it is not begun with a 'quiet time'.

Many superstitions begin for us as very good habits, or simple matters of traditional practice which do not have any great significance. However, because we are even in this twentieth century religious people, we overlay these things with religious significance. Religious feelings come to be attached to them and in an almost intangible way they come to have a special significance, even though the exact character of the significance cannot be identified. Religious feelings are part of our human make-up which we bring to our Christian faith, but Christianity is fundamentally ethical and opposed to superstition.

140

III ACTIVITY SUGGESTIONS

It follows from what has been said that there are really two kinds of activity work to be done in relation to this book. In order to show how this might work out I shall go over in a little detail two examples, one taken from the second part of the book and one that is not treated in the book, outlining the questions to be asked and how they might be handled. By taking an example which has been discussed in this book already it will be possible to see how the book might be used by a teacher or group leader to draw up further activity suggestions and to check the results of the work. By taking an example not discussed in the book, a teacher or group will be able to launch themselves for further independent work.

In approaching and planning this work, readers are advised to remember the following points. The work for the first question (which considers the meaning for the New Testament writers) can be done individually as well as in a group. Help can be obtained from commentaries and, for the examples covered, from part II of this book. However, the second question (which considers the meaning for the present day) is much better handled in a group where different backgrounds and knowledge are brought to bear.

The work for the first question takes time. It involves looking up things, reading passages carefully and thinking over the various questions. In a school or house group situation it could be regarded as preparatory work for a group discussion.

For the second question we are concerned with the meaning for today and it would be good to have people in the discussion who could contribute directly from their particular competence. These could be a doctor, a psychologist, a sociologist, a scientist such as a physicist or a chemist, or a clergyman. They could then be asked how they understood the way the world worked today from the standpoint of their profession and in relation to the conclusions which had been arrived at from the first question. In a school situation, where it might not be possible to have such a variety of people involved in the discussion, different roles of sociologist, psychologist, etc. might be assigned to different students, and they could then be asked to contribute to the

141

discussion from the standpoint of their assigned role. It would be useful for students to have time for prior preparation if this method were used.

1

The Temptation of Jesus

Text:

Matthew 4:1–11; Mark 1:12–13; Luke 4:1–13. (*See also pages 19ff.*)

A. What did it mean to the New Testament writers?

This story occurs in the first three gospels and we should therefore work through the four questions listed below. Refer to the discussion of this story in the second part of this book to check your answers.

(i) What is the place of the story in the synoptic tradition as a whole?

It comes in all three gospels in roughly the same place. Thus it was generally thought of as at, or just prior to the beginning of Jesus' public ministry. What does this imply about the function of the story in the gospels?

(ii) What is the place of the story within the particular gospel, and what tendencies of interpretation are revealed by its place?

To help you answer this question the order of events at the beginning of each of the gospels is as follows:

Matthew Genealogy (1:1–17), Birth of Jesus (1:18–25), The Magi (2:1–12), Flight into Egypt (2:13–23), Ministry of John the Baptist (3:1–12), Baptism of Jesus (3:13–17), Temptation (4:1–11), Jesus begins his ministry (4:12–25).

Mark Title (1:1), John the Baptist's testimony (1:2–8), Baptism of Jesus (1:9–11), Temptation (1:12–13), Jesus begins his ministry (1:14–15), Some disciples are called (1:16–20).

Luke Prologue (1:1–4), Infancy narratives (1:5–2:52), John the Baptist's work and imprisonment (3:1–20), Baptism of Jesus (3:21–22), Genealogy (3:23–38), Temptation (4:1–13), A summary comment on Jesus' popularity (4:14–15).

What is the significance of the order of events: John the Baptist's ministry, the baptism of Jesus, the temptation?

Why does Luke place the genealogy between the baptism and the temptation, while Matthew and Mark have these two close together?

(iii) What interpretative imagery is used in the story itself?

What details are common to all three accounts? Notice that Mark does not give detailed information about the temptations as do Matthew and Luke.

What details are common to Matthew and Luke?

—The temptations are directed to belief in Jesus as the Son of God.

—The temptations use scripture, but in a way that is pretty clearly not approved of by the gospel writers.

—Jesus' sonship is asserted in terms of: trust in God for daily sustenance; not testing God; worshipping God.

(iv) What is the relationship between the structural position of the story (question ii) and the imagery (question iii)?

How far is the picture of the 'Son of God' in the answers to the temptations a model for Christians generally, and how far is the picture in the temptations put to Jesus a counterexample?

Now, can you identify a general line of interpretation in these accounts? What did the writers want their readers to believe and to do in the light of this story?

Is this an account of a subjective experience of Jesus?

How far is this meant to be a once-for-all event, and how far is it meant to be an example for Christians?

B. What does it mean today?

How does this experience of Jesus relate to our understanding of the world and of human experience today? What would be the view of a psychologist or sociologist?

What difference does it make that the story refers to an event two thousand years ago?

How would you express today the interpretative thrust identified in answer to question A?

2
Jesus Feeds a Crowd of Four Thousand
Text:

Matthew 15:32–39; Mark 8:1–10.

A. What did it mean to the New Testament writers?

(i) What is the place of the story in the synoptic tradition as a whole?
Compare the similar story at Matthew 14:13–21; Mark 6:32–44;
Luke 9:10–17. See also the narrative in Matthew 16:5–12; Mark
8:14–21. The feedings are not connected in this way in Luke.

(ii) What is the place of the story within the particular gospel, and
what tendencies of interpretation are revealed by its place?
For Matthew read through the gospel to chapter 17 in the New
English Bible or some easy-to-read modern translation. Notice how
this story is part of the final build-up to the confession at Caesarea
Philippi.
For Mark do the same quick reading exercise as for Matthew, going
up to chapter 9. Notice that there is less teaching material in this part
of Mark as compared with Matthew, and that the miracle stories are
grouped together by Mark.

(iii) What interpretative imagery is used in the story itself? What
are the details common to both Matthew and Mark? What details
are found only in one or the other?

(iv) What is the relationship between the structural position of the
story (question ii) and the imagery (question iii)?
Now, can you indentify a general line of interpretation in these accounts? What did the writers want their readers to believe and to do
in the light of this story?

B. What does it mean today?
How does this story relate to our understanding of the world and of
human experience today?
What difference does it make that the story relates to an incident
two thousand years ago? Is the story so intimately bound up with
Jesus' own life in the interpretation of the gospel writers that it cannot
have any direct relevance to the present day?
How does the interpretative line of the New Testament writers
work out today?